Your Leadership Story

Use Your Story To Energize, Inspire, And Motivate

Timothy J. Tobin

16pt

Copyright Page from the Original Book

Your Leadership Story

Berrett-Koehler Publishers, Inc.
1333 Broadway, Suite 1000
Oakland, CA 94612-1921
Tel: (510) 817-2277, Fax: (510) 817-2278
www.bkconnection.com

Ordering information for print editions
Quantity sales. Special discounts are available on quantity purchases by cor-
porations, associations, and others. For details, contact the "Special Sales
Department" at the Berrett-Koehler address above.
Individual sales. Berrett-Koehler publications are available through most
bookstores. They can also be ordered directly from Berrett-Koehler: Tel:
(800) 929-2929; Fax: (802) 864-7626; www.bkconnection.com
Orders for college textbook/course adoption use. Please contact Berrett-
Koehler: Tel: (800) 929-2929; Fax: (802) 864-7626.
Orders by U.S. trade bookstores and wholesalers. Please contact Ingram
Publisher Services, Tel: (800) 509-4887; Fax: (800) 838-1149; E-mail:
customer.service@ingrampublisherservices.com; or visit www.ingram
publisherservices.com/Ordering for details about electronic ordering.

Berrett-Koehler and the BK logo are registered trademarks of Berrett-Koehler
Publishers, Inc.

First Edition
Hardcover print edition ISBN 978-1-62656-294-3
PDF e-book ISBN 978-1-62656-295-0
IDPF e-book ISBN 978-1-62656-296-7

2015-1

INTERIOR DESIGN: Valerie Brewster. EDITOR: Elissa Rabellino.

COVER DESIGN: Barbara Haines. PROOFREADER: Henrietta Bensussen.

INDEX: Paula C. Durbin-Westby. PRODUCTION SERVICE: Linda Jupiter
Productions.

TABLE OF CONTENTS

More Praise for Your Leadership Story

"The counsel of ancient wisdom is to know thyself. To be effective as a leader, you not only have to know thyself, you have to share thyself. The ability to know and tell your leadership story is critical to engaging others to get bigger things done. Tim Tobin has written a handbook that will help you learn how to do that."
—**Scott Eblin, author of** *The Next Level* **and** *Overworked and Overwhelmed*

"Tim Tobin talks about the importance of self-awareness and its crucial place in our action-oriented world. The ability to be self-aware as one moves upward in the organizational hierarchy is critical and often lacking. Read this book and apply the exercises and questions to yourself. Guaranteed to raise your self-awareness quotient and provide you with a way of more effectively developing your team."

—**Beverly Kaye, founder, Career Systems International, and coauthor of** *Help Them Grow or Watch Them Go* **and** *Love 'Em or Lose 'Em*

"*Your Leadership Story* is a wonderful book that helps you reflect, understand, and develop your own leadership capabilities in a personal way. Everyone who leads teams, projects, or an organization should read this book."
—**Josh Bersin, Principal and founder, Bersin by Deloitte**

"Knowing my life's story and constantly updating it gives me the information I need to know who I am and enables me to connect with those I lead. Tim Tobin's book tells me how to do it."
—**Robert M. Tobias, Professor, Key Executive Leadership Program, American University**

"Much is being written on how to become a better, more authentic leader. There is literally an ocean of recommendations—many of which are difficult to understand and use. In *Your Leadership Story,* Tim Tobin cuts through the leadership noise and identifies an understandable and effective way to become a better leader—by truly understanding and effectively communicating your own leadership story."

—Walter McFarland, coauthor of ***Choosing Change***

"Great leadership and skillful storytelling are nearly synonymous. *Your Leadership Story* is provocative, filled with fresh insights, and immensely practical. Tim Tobin brings wonderful clarity to the leadership/storytelling connections."

—Jim Loehr, bestselling author and cofounder, Human Performance Institute

"Your leadership journey is a powerful tool for motivating yourself and others. Tim Tobin shows you how to turn that journey into a compelling story. Don't miss this one!"

—**Steve Arneson, PhD, author of** *Bootstrap Leadership* **and** *What Your Boss Really Wants from You*

"Tim Tobin's focus on perceptions of leaders—their own and those they seek to influence—speaks eloquently to the point. This book provides leaders with sage advice and skills in crafting, aligning, and communicating the message they speak with the message they model. Powerful in their simplicity, leadership stories, when taken to heart and mind, can help you accelerate your leadership effectiveness."

—**Victoria J. Marsick, Professor, Department of Organization & Leadership, and Codirector, J.M. Huber Institute for Learning in Organizations, Teachers College, Columbia University**

For Chase, Finley, and Sara—
You are my greatest source of inspiration and you provide the greatest meaning to my story each day.

FOREWORD

Leadership starts with you. To be truly effective, you need to know who you are and who you wish to be as a leader. You have to have a clear sense of what moves you to lead. You need a strong inner compass to ensure that you are consistently making the right choices. Without this inner clarity, you'll be pulled in directions that are unlikely to harness your potential or the potential of those who follow you. Metaphorically, it's like navigating a new city without the map app on your phone. You'll experience one misstep after another. You will not arrive at the aspirational end point each of us wishes to achieve over our lifetime.

So the journey to leading begins with you—discovering and making the most of personal passions, preempting costly mistakes through core values and remembering lessons learned in your past. You have to know your own leadership story. This singular insight is why Tim Tobin's book must be at the top of your reading list. It is a paradox, but if you wish to lead, you have to take a step back. You need to reflect on what means the most to you and to those you lead.

In my own work with executives and managers, I am surprised at how many have given far too little thought to who they are or who they wish to be as leaders. It is shocking. I say this because I know the price they are paying for this lack of insight. Instead of leading, they end up spending their days managing at best. They are pulled by whatever demands their immediate attention. They will also make poor choices because they lack an inner sense of what's the right thing to do. They'll make compromises when they shouldn't. They'll repeat their mistakes. They will all too rarely articulate their aspirations since these are drowned out by a "ticking the boxes" mentality. As a result, these individuals lack vision and consequently lack the capacity to inspire. The ultimate price they pay for this lack of insight into themselves? They never realize their personal potential. Quite a number plateau in their careers, or, worse yet, they derail.

What Tim Tobin has done so beautifully is to provide a structured means for you to explore the essential dimensions of your personal leadership story. I will say that his book is the most thorough guide to crafting such stories that I have read. He takes you step-by-step. By deploying wide-ranging and provocative questions, he will have you reflecting deeply on what has shaped you as a leader and where you wish to go as a leader. I like to think of his book as the equivalent of the Mayo Clinic's Executive Physical for leadership stories—every dimension of you as a leader will be explored!

But why are these personal stories so essential to leadership? There is a funny thing that happens when you have to create a story for yourself. It forces you to powerfully clarify what is most meaningful and inspirational to you. You'll also come to realize that you really do possess an inner set of values. These are touchstones for your mental well-being. If you stray from them for long, something deep inside will disturb you over and over again. With clarity, you will be less seduced by the immediate distractions that take you away from your gifts and the accomplishments you wish to achieve. You will be less seduced by choices that have a short-term payoff (in reality, a false sense of accomplishment) but have a longer-term and expensive cost. As you go public with your story and share it widely, you'll experience a greater sense of personal accountability to live up to it. In other words, you will find yourself not only telling your story but also living it far more consistently! You will discover how it gives you so much more clarity when you are confronted with daily crossroad choices.

There's another big advantage to having a rich leadership story. It will help your associates to remember the right choices they need to make every day. They will be reminded of what is most meaningful about the work you do as a team and the values and parameters that should guide every important decision. Why is that? Pioneering work in neuroscience and memory is revealing that stories engage us far more profoundly than PowerPoint presentations or abstract discussions or value and mission statements. They are incredibly sticky. We easily retain in our memories the moving personal stories of others. Witness those told thousands of years ago by the world's great religious leaders. Their stories, rich in lessons and guidelines, remain vivid today. We can recall them with ease.

What also makes this book special is that you will be learning from one of the most passionate individuals in the field of leadership. Tim loves leadership. He has lived it, taught it, studied it, and coached it. He has spent years learning the methodology of constructing effective leadership stories. This passion comes through in the purpose of this book: to help individuals see and experience their potential to truly lead.

In sum, your investment in this book will expand your conception of who you are and can be as a leader. In the long run, it will transform your impact over your career. I wish you a wonderful journey of self-discovery.

Jay A. Conger
Chairman
Kravis Leadership Institute
Claremont McKenna College

PREFACE

Most of my professional working life has been focused on leadership development. I studied it in school. I have helped a variety of large and small organizations build award-winning leadership programs. I have worked with leaders across industries. I have had the opportunity to work with top leaders and world-class leadership speakers. I have led small teams and big teams. And I have observed others doing the same. I have also been fortunate to have some great mentors. And I have been equally fortunate to coach other leaders. I am a student of leadership. I have dedicated my life to it, and I have learned a great deal along the way.

If you look closely, you might say I have leadership coming out of my ears. (It's really not as uncomfortable as it sounds.) So as you launch into this book, you might be thinking, this guy must be a leadership genius. He must be (sound of horns) The Perfect Leader.

And do you know what? You would be wrong. OK, perfect is probably not a fair or realistic goal for anyone to strive for when it comes to leadership. There are just too many moving parts to leadership for anyone to be able to nail it all the time.

So to be fair, let's say the target is to be a consistently great leader—the kind of leader who inspires and motivates others. Someone who leaves a positive, lasting impression. That seems more realistic and more attainable.

Whatever the end measure, truth be told, I still don't get leadership right all the time. Heck, I'd settle for pretty darn good on some days.

Let me pause right there for a second. Why would anyone want to strive for leadership greatness? If it is to feed the ego, reconsider: it rarely ends in greatness. If the motivation is more altruistic in nature—to help others, guide them, develop them—you will find consistently greater fruits of your leadership labor.

If I can spend all this time immersed in the topic of leadership and not always get it right, how are people who are focused on countless responsibilities other than leadership supposed to get it right? That is an awful lot to expect. I've encountered great leadership, and I've seen great leaders have off days as well. To me, though, it's all the possibilities that make leadership so fun. That's right—leadership should be fun. But let's not underestimate the level of effort, planning, and development that our leaders require if they are to be at their best for those they lead.

Success at one point in one's career does not guarantee success at another point. I have seen in far too many instances that highly capable technical experts are promoted to a leadership position—with little or no leadership training. And they are expected to continue on their path to excellence. Unfortunately, what I've also seen is that sometimes that works out and sometimes it doesn't. I'm not much of a betting man, but I don't like those odds.

We've all heard the "Leadership is a journey" metaphor, and it is fair to say that I am still on my journey and you are still on yours. In fact, this book was born out of the realization that I've still got a lot to learn. I'm also at a point where I have a lot to share.

I wrote this book primarily for emerging leaders. Look, I realize that not everyone has the opportunity to attend a multiday leadership program or to have a personal leadership coach. Both of those take time and can cost a lot of money. But it doesn't mean you should be left to your own devices to just figure leadership out. Unfortunately, for any number of reasons, that is far too often the case.

Emerging leaders likely have the most questions about leadership and the fewest resources to support their development. You should think of this book as being like a class in leadership—not the dry, theoretical stuff (don't tell any of my professors I said that) but the real, practical stuff. In fact, consider this your personal class in which to become more aware of your leadership capacity and to improve it.

And for you current leaders who think you have it all figured out, you might want to give this book a good read because you might be surprised by what you find. Of course, any leaders who are looking to better understand who they are as a leader, as well as leaders going through a career transition, will benefit as well.

I wanted to do something to help enable more people to have greater success as leaders—not simply for them but also for those they lead. To create all-around better experiences. To develop more people. To—as the book's subtitle suggests—energize, inspire, and motivate others to be their best. And leadership is about people, to be sure, but it is also about delivering better results for the business in the process.

If you've read this far, I hope you have an interest in becoming a better leader. I would love to contribute to your journey in some way. So we're in this together now. You'll see that I ask a lot of questions throughout the book. I would encourage you to avoid a superficial treatment of the questions and activities, and instead to reflect upon them deeply. Forget about the rule against writing in a book—if you've got an insight, don't let it get away.

As with many things, you can expect to get only what you give. If you are willing to challenge yourself with some of the questions and look more deeply within yourself, you will gain far greater—possibly even transformational—benefits. I tend to lean toward optimism. With a greater understanding of your leadership story, you'll find that the best is yet to come.

Timothy J. Tobin
Washington, D.C.

INTRODUCTION

What is your leadership story? More important, who is the author of your leadership story, you ... or someone else? This book examines why it is important for you to be the author of your own leadership story and how you can best communicate its value.

Let me tell you about one of my clients. I'll call him Bob. Bob was a self-confident, solid technical expert in his field—it doesn't matter which one. Although he had been a manager for a while, his successes, he felt, were catching up with him. He was being asked to take on more duties. He had never felt the need to hire a coach before, but when we talked, here are some of the revealing concerns he confided in me.

- Am I taking on too many responsibilities, too much? How do I know when to say when?
- Can I handle an increased leadership role beyond my technical role?

- I am not sure that I handle every managerial or project leadership role as best as I should.
- Right now, I seem to be trying to balance my technical expertise with the managerial role and project leadership I am being asked to handle.
- What does it mean to be a leader—I mean, a real leader who can maintain that balance?
- How do you lead people who have been peers and friends and lunch buddies?
- What do I do myself, and what do I delegate, and when do I know the difference?
- How do I balance the new work roles and my personal life?
- Others have done it. I'm confident that I can, but I just need some definition. No one wants to be an example of the Peter Principle.

I've known and worked with thousands of Bobs. And Jills. As you go through the steps of this book—yes, it's about a practical process—we will visit with Bob as he faces each step. As a reader, you can get inside Bob's head or imagine that you are he. His story is quite typical of successful people who are taking on more responsibility and seek out someone like me.

Your leadership story is the collection of events, perspectives, and behaviors that represent who you are as a leader. It evolves from your unique experiences. Your leadership story is not like that of the person in the next department. Hers is different; neither story is right or wrong. Your leadership story communicates the message of identity: who you are as a leader, what you believe in, what drives you and defines you as a leader, and how you act.

If I don't know about you as a person, then I don't know about you as a leader. And whether preparing to be a leader for the first time or an established leader with many years of experience, every leader has a story.

All leadership stories should be dynamic. They are colorful depictions of events that provide a snapshot in time, yet they are works in progress. They energize, inspire, and motivate. Stories illustrate and reinforce key points and provide meaning and relevance. They help us to learn, impart a lesson, and communicate a message. Stories help us to make an emotional connection; and, told well, stories are compelling and memorable.

This book is about making your leadership story compelling and memorable. This is not about how to spit out a 15-second elevator speech.

I have been directly responsible for the development of thousands of leaders across a variety of industries and levels, and each leader has his or her own leadership story. Unfortunately, too often, leaders do not spend time thinking about or planning their story. It is given little thought or attention, and it is left to chance. Leaders who take a proactive role in understanding and communicating their story have increased capacity, stronger connections, greater self-awareness, greater authenticity, and better preparation to make routine and unanticipated decisions.

This book teaches you how to make your leadership story memorable by providing you with guidance for you to become the writer, director, and star of the story. Better yet, let's make it an epic.

Whom Is This Book For, and How Should It Be Used?

This isn't a book where you will find validation of how excellent you think you are. Rather, it's about taking an honest look in the mirror and discovering how your story is perceived by others. After all, wouldn't you like to know how others see your leadership? Wouldn't that be helpful to your career development?

Most leaders are much more than what they appear to be. This book is meant to help you to be good, not to look good. You need to delve below the surface of your leadership and uncover the *why* that underlies it. If you go deeper within—to what you value as a leader, how you think and how you act—and move beyond what you think others want to hear to what you truly believe, this book and process has the potential to be transformational.

It is for all current or aspiring leaders who want to take control of their own leadership story. If, as a leader, you are interested simply in getting tasks done more efficiently, then this book may not be for you. It's not about project management.

Instead, it introduces a process to facilitate the self-reflection required for you to understand your leadership story. Included is a collection of activities and tips to help you build, shape, and communicate your story.

If you are interested in making a deeper, stronger emotional connection with those you lead, and you want to find greater energy and inspiration as a leader, then this book is for you. It is about developing a positive effect on the people you lead. Do you know whether your people resent or crave your leadership? Wouldn't you want people to crave it?

You cannot fake leadership. It must be sincere and real and reflect who you are. You must search your soul for what you truly believe and not just massage what you want others to see or hear.

Chapter I will outline types of leadership and lack thereof.

You may choose to simply skim through the steps of this process with an eye toward identifying how you look or sound as a leader. If so, the result will likely be a superficial treatment of your leadership story. In life, in career, when does doing something halfway feel good, and when does it ever create added value? In *Creating Personal Presence,* Dianna Booher argues that personal presence is composed of four dimensions: Look, Talk, Think, and Act. She notes that most people emphasize the Look and Talk dimensions and assume that they are who you are. She points out that the Think and Act dimensions are the most important, and the most difficult, because they exist at a deeper level.[1] That is the level I'm talking about here.

For this to be transformational, you're going to need to do some soul-searching. And it might be uncomfortable at times. The real value: it's transformational not just for you but also for those you lead.

The Parts of This Book

The book is made up of steps and chapters. When it comes to your leadership story, there are 10 steps—five to understand your story and five to communicate it. Each step guides you through questions, activities, and tips to give you a deeper understanding of your story and help you ultimately to become a better leader. Although all of the steps are meant to fit together, you may find it necessary to spend more time on one step than another.

In chapter 1, we try to define just what leadership is. What enhances it and what compromises it? Why do others sometimes have a view of your leadership that is very different from what you see in the mirror? We also meet Bob. He will be with us throughout the book as he tackles each step, right along with you.

In chapter 2, we focus on defining and understanding what the current and ideal versions of your leadership story are. Each step in this chapter deals with a different story element; it includes an overview of the element and why it is important, five reflective questions, five activities designed to further create self-awareness and drive action, and three quick tips.

Stories take place over time, and they have a beginning, middle, and end. When it comes to your leadership story, the narrative arc is that point in your career when it all comes together. In chapter 3, you will have the opportunity to identify and reflect upon where you are on your narrative arc, as well as the people and events that have had the greatest influence on who you are as a leader.

In chapter 4, we focus on how you can best communicate your leadership story. The steps take you through knowing your message and audience, looking for and maximizing moments of truth, understanding the role of actions and other nonverbal communication, and enlisting others to help you tell your leadership story. Each step provides an overview of the topic and why it is important. I also include reflective questions to help you think about how to communicate your leadership story, strategies to help you refine the message of your leadership story, and a short anecdote to illustrate that aspect of storytelling.

I end the book with a conclusion and resources. The conclusion ties all of the concepts together and provides final thoughts for you to consider. It provides an opportunity for you to look back at the whole process of understanding and communicating your story. My hope is that at the conclusion of this book, you are better prepared for challenges and rewards of leadership. Further, I hope that you are more inspired and that you have a greater ability to inspire those you lead.

The resources section provides a quick guide to the activities you can do yourself and those to give to others. It also gathers in one central place the reflective questions designed to help you understand and communicate your story, and the tips from each step in the process.

The perspective and activities in this book are meant to establish a process for reflection, to put in place an understanding that will help you avoid blind spots and become the author of your leadership story. After reading this book and working through some of the reflective questions and activities, you will have a better understanding of the current and ideal versions of your leadership story. You will also have strategies to communicate your leadership story.

So, if you are ready, let's get started.

CHAPTER I

Just What Is Leadership?

In this chapter, I want to help you understand what I call *the ecology of leadership.* Obviously, someone cannot be much of a leader if no one is there to be led. So it's a delicate environment of projects, priorities, and plans as well as emotions, sensitivities, and ambitions.

President Eisenhower once commented, "Leadership is the art of getting someone to do something you want done because he wants to do it." Ike's approach to delegation could be called subtle. But to him, delegation was an important skill and a big deal. It surely served him well in Europe as he dealt with many big egos to lead the Allied effort in World War II.

A Word about Perceptions

Speaking of Ike, we typically don't think of him as having had a big ego.

Supreme Allied commander, president of Columbia University, general of the Army, president of the United States. That's a résumé that would enable anyone's ego to balloon. But not Eisenhower. He was awesome and not awesome at the same time.

Likewise, it is important for all of us to understand how we are perceived by others and where that is consistent with our self-perceptions. If there is misalignment between the two, it is important to understand why that is. As the introduction implies, this book's process and steps are not intended to reaffirm to you that you are just so awesome right now. In a few paragraphs, you will meet Bob and watch his lunch mates tell him how not awesome he really is. It is a shocker for him.

What Is Your Leadership Story?

The truth is, you are only as good a leader as people think you are. That's hard to accept if you wear awesomeness on your sleeve. A self-review of your leadership would contain inherent flaws, and too often leaders attempt to rationalize their behavior. According to the book *Leadership and Self-Deception,* by the Arbinger Institute, leaders can blind themselves to their true motivations and capabilities.[2] Without a review from others, it is unlikely that our self-perception is accurate—whether positive or critical. Rarely is our own perception exactly right. And that has implications for our ability to lead others effectively.

Our awareness and acceptance of our imperfections is the pathway to excellence. To that end, this book establishes a system of checks and balances to help you to truly understand who you are as a leader, based not only on your perceptions but also on the perceptions and interpretations of others. You may not like what you hear. It may not align with your self-image. But it is critical to fully understanding your story. Think of it this way: The value added is balance.

Your leadership story is the intersection between what you believe your story to be and others' interpretations. It is reflected in what you say and do as well as how others perceive and interpret what you say and do as a leader. And to add to the complexity, others' interpretations may not be accurate. Or worse, their motivations may not support your story.

This paradox of who owns your story is a constant struggle. Are you the primary author? Or does your story live in the interpretations of others? The answer is yes to both. If you do not take primary authorship of your story, it will be crafted exclusively through the perceptions of others. That will not be a very accurate autobiography. The following figure illustrates the importance of understanding and aligning your leadership story with the perceptions of others. It also shows the problems of being misunderstood.

VARIATIONS (OR INTERPRETATIONS)
OF YOUR LEADERSHIP STORY

	Accurate	I Insecure, humble, arrogant, clueless	II Authentic, genuine, aligned, reliable
Others' Perceptions	Inaccurate	IV Inconsistent, unaware, unreliable, erratic	III Disregarded, hidden, unknown, overlooked
		Inaccurate	Accurate

Self-Perceptions

Your leadership story currently exists somewhere within the quadrants above. Each is described in detail below. Your story can manifest itself positively or negatively in each of the quadrants. Your objective is to understand your leadership story, work to get it to where you want it to be, and make sure that others are aligned with it.

QUADRANT 1

This is a difficult place for leaders to find themselves in. It suggests that others know you better than you know yourself. On a slightly positive note, leaders here do not believe in themselves, nor do they believe that they have great attributes as a leader, and this may show itself as being humble. But even humility has a dark side: over time, others will eventually not believe in you, either.

Jeff lived in Q1. Everyone thought he was great, but he was quick to deflect praise. He would always say, "No, no. I didn't do that. My team did." Noble indeed. People appreciated his humility, but eventually he convinced others that he really couldn't do it, and that fate became part of his story. In a sense, he wrote it himself.

Ben was a leader who ran into this challenge. He was viewed by many as humble. He did not take credit for his expertise and leadership capabilities. When others gave him credit, he was quick to deflect it and say, "Oh, I'm not sure I did that." He was admired by many, and then, over time, others began to question his abilities. It began simply enough, with a few peers and leaders saying, "I'm not sure," about his abilities. Although his story never left Quadrant I, it quickly transitioned from humility to a question of capability. He had effectively talked others into not believing in him. An adage comes to mind: If you believe you can't do something, you are probably right.

Another type exists in this quadrant. They are the leaders who are narcissistic, self-important, or overconfident. Leaders here think they are awesome—and they aren't afraid to let others know it through their words or actions. However, awesome is not how they are perceived by others. In either case, these leaders either are clueless or simply don't care how they are showing up as a leader. Your solution, if you find yourself to be in this quadrant, is to seek feedback and listen to others. You may find it beneficial to do a skills audit and to work on your executive presence.

QUADRANT 2

Using the story as a metaphor, this quadrant is known as a leader's true story. Leaders in this quadrant have a good understanding of their leadership story, and others do as well. Leaders here are viewed as authentic—what you see is what you get. They are genuine. They know their strengths and areas for development, and they tend to be willing to enlist the support of others.

Even if these leaders' stories have negative attributes, they are aware of this and either take corrective action individually or are conscious of when and how to supplement their skills. But leaders here should not get too comfortable. If you find yourself in this space, you should continue to reflect, be self-aware, and enlist others to tell their story.

Randy may not have had all the answers, but he was willing to bring in others to help. He had great ideas, but he knew he wasn't an expert in everything. His go-to phrase was "What do you think?" You felt like you knew him on a personal level and that he cared about you. And he was passionate about the work he was doing.

QUADRANT 3

Leaders here are, well, hidden. They have a good understanding of their story, but no one else does. Because others don't know who these leaders are, they tend to be overlooked.

If you know your story and it is negative, you may lack credibility and will have some work to do to become a better leader. If you know who you are as a leader and it is positive, you need to become better known as a leader. If you are in this quadrant, focus on building your network, get involved throughout the organization in projects and initiatives, and enlist others to tell your leadership story.

Jeremy was a leader who fit this description. He was new to the organization, fresh out of graduate school. He had a lot of bright ideas but no way of sharing them. It wasn't his style to aggressively assert himself, and he didn't want to come across as bragging or trying to take charge. But eventually he became frustrated. He and I worked on ways to build his internal network and get involved in projects to showcase what he was capable of.

QUADRANT 4

These leaders are inconsistent and unclear at best; they are erratic and unreliable at worst. Just as in Quadrant I, such leaders lack self-awareness. They lack thought and reflection about who they are as leaders, what they value, and what they stand for.

Many leaders here have not taken the time to understand who they are or what they believe in as a leader. To make this quadrant more directly personal to you, no one else knows you or what you believe in, either. People may follow you because you are the boss, but they are skeptical and reluctant to do so.

If you find yourself in this quadrant, you should begin by understanding your leadership story. As a starting point, focus on what you believe in and value as a leader. The good news is that almost any action you take toward understanding, aligning, or communicating your leadership story is a step in the right direction.

Sam was an established leader within the organization, due in large part to his technical knowledge. Sometimes he wanted to get into the details and sometimes he didn't. He would assign tasks and follow up on some but not others. None of Sam's direct reports knew what to expect from him, nor did some of his peers. How do you think his team felt? He never thought about how this was affecting his team—creating low morale, poor performance, and a sense of uncertainty. Others viewed him as volatile and inconsistent.

Types of Leadership

What type of leadership do you want to master? What leadership style do you aspire to? You need to think about what type of leader you want to be. And here is the fun part about leadership: there is not one single best way to lead.

The choice is yours. Choose the kind of leadership, or combination thereof, that best suits you and that you aspire to. The purpose of this activity is not merely to increase self-awareness. It will help you to consider the ultimate goals of leadership so that you keep in mind the importance of your leadership for the greater good. The result will be a more meaningful goal—or set of goals—that brings fulfillment to you and those you lead.

There are many types of leadership. What does leadership mean to you? What is the role and purpose of a leader? As you think about your own definition of leadership, some of the words you used may have given you a clue as to what style of leadership you gravitate toward. Did you use words such as *help* or *serve others?* Did you talk about developing others? Do you look at leadership as a process? Is it interactive? With whom? As you think about the kind of leader you want to be, consider the various types of leadership described in the table below.

TYPES OF LEADERSHIP

Type of Leadership	Illustrative Perspectives
Servant leadership	Robert Greenleaf, Ken Blanchard, Mark Miller
Purpose-driven leadership	Bill George, Clayton Christensen
Positive leadership	Robert Quinn, Ryan Quinn, Kim Cameron
Appreciative Inquiry leadership	David Cooperrider, Diana Whitney, Ed Schein

Stewardship leadership	Peter Block, Nelson Mandela
Conversations That Matter leadership	Meg Wheatley, Bev Kaye, Sharon Jordan-Evans, Juanita Brown
Peer-to-peer leadership	Mila Baker, Bill George
Benevolent dictatorship	So many examples
Command-and-control leadership	Some very famous examples

Toward a Balanced Leadership Story for You

This book is about getting your leadership story straight. It is about facing the realities of your leadership story from multiple angles. It is about understanding who you are as a leader and who you want to be. It is also about understanding and aligning your beliefs as a leader with the perceptions of others—that critical balance. In short, *Your Leadership Story* is about understanding, aligning, and communicating who you are as a leader.

Two Big Questions

Chapter 1 concerns two important questions, so let's try to answer them.

WHAT MAKES GREAT LEADERSHIP?

Many definitions of leadership exist—too many to mention here. What does great leadership mean to you? And what does it mean in the context of your organization?

Look around you at the various leaders you deal with regularly. What do they do that is inspiring? Uninspiring? There are plenty of examples of great leaders and bad leaders. Wherever you stand on the spectrum of great-to-poor leaders and whatever your definition of leadership is, I would have one question for you: How is that working for you? If everything is going perfectly, keep up the good work. For most leaders, there are opportunities for improvement somewhere in their skill set.

Despite the complexity of leadership, there seem to be some common attributes, skills, and characteristics among great leaders. Leaders have to be technically competent. But technical competence can be both a hindrance and a requirement to be a great leader.

I refer to technical competence as a critical part of your leadership foundation because you have to have technical competence and understand the business you are in before you can be a leader. At the same time, as you take on leadership responsibilities, you will have to let go of some of your technical responsibilities—that which got you here—in order to embrace leadership. You need to take time to understand the various aspects of the business you are in, the competitive landscape, and the operating environment in order to make good, fundamentally sound, and relevant business decisions.

Technical competence can be a barrier to great leadership for two reasons. First, being technically competent does not automatically ensure leadership competence. I have seen this firsthand on numerous occasions where a perfectly capable employee gets promoted into a leadership position and fails as a leader. Second, leaders with technical expertise may have a difficult time letting go of their technical responsibilities. I have seen leaders continue to spend time on aspects of their job that they should delegate. Great leaders need to focus on leadership.

Great leadership requires providing vision and direction. It requires motivating and inspiring people to work toward the vision. It requires developing other people. And it requires achieving results. In short, leadership is about people. Your ability to connect with people can make all the difference between great and poor leadership. Where this gets particularly complex is that different people have different needs, and those needs may shift over time, along with a host of other changing variables. Leadership is a dynamic, moving target that requires you to be thoughtful and prepared in your approach. Your leadership story serves as an anchor and foundation for your actions as a leader.

Great leaders have a plan, and also they are great improvisers. Just as a good actor has to improvise onstage if something unplanned happens, great business leaders, as improvisers, are the actor, writer, and director of their story. They must act in the moment. As writer, they must initiate ideas. And as director, they must provide a bigger view and facilitate room for ideas, creativity, and action.

WHY FOCUS ON YOUR LEADERSHIP STORY?

You are the actor, writer, and director of your leadership story. You act in the moment, initiate ideas, provide a bigger view, and allow for ideas and creativity. Understanding and communicating your leadership story can be quite powerful. It provides clarity around what you stand for as a leader. It keeps alive the people, values, and life lessons that you hold dear. It gives you the power of influence and authenticity by allowing you to match your words and your actions. It allows you to build trust. Trust leads to credibility.

By helping you to understand what has shaped you as a leader, your leadership story can make the strong emotional connection that is necessary to inspire and motivate others. It can also be a useful tool with which to impart knowledge and lessons to others—to help them learn from the experiences that have shaped your leadership story. And it provides you and others with insights into what you hold important as a leader.

By understanding your leadership story, you will have greater self-awareness and fewer blind spots. It will also provide a starting point for you as you continue to develop as a leader. It will guide you in modifying your story so that you can be a better leader. When you effectively communicate your leadership story, you and others will have clarity about your expectations as a leader.

Leadership is a journey that involves the past, the present, and the future. Once upon a time, your leadership story was a blank page filled with hopes, dreams, opportunities, and inspiration. For many, those hopes and dreams included being a great leader. As you have realized some hopes and dreams, and have learned more through experience about what makes a great leader, perhaps new or revised ideas around being a great leader have sprung up.

What has contributed to the evolution of your notions about leadership? What has supported you in your personal quest to be a great leader? What has inhibited you from being your best? Looking ahead, what are you prepared to do to be the best leader you can be?

My six-year-old daughter recently told me something profound and relevant to understanding our leadership story. She said, "First you plant a seed. Then you nourish it. Then it sprouts. Then it grows. Finally, it turns into a flower."

Our nourishment for growth and development consists of reflection, action, and insights. Let's face it—we operate in a very action-oriented environment. We spend more time on action and results that reward us, and far less time on thinking and reflecting. Reflection is a process of understanding what happened and why. It creates self-awareness. A lack of self-awareness leads to blind spots, and at the least it puts you at a disadvantage as a leader.

Who's got time for this reflection and self-awareness? I would restate that: Who has time to get leadership wrong? When you combine self-awareness with a willingness to stretch outside your comfort zone, you will see the greatest breakthroughs and maximize your leadership potential.

Learning plays a key role in developing your story. Reflection is about asking yourself questions. It may require thinking differently and taking action in order to build capability. Once you have mastered your leadership story, you will make stronger connections and inspire, energize, and motivate those you lead. You will be a better leader.

When I run workshops for leaders, at the end of the session, I ask the group a simple question: "So what?" So what did you learn from this? And so what are you going to do with it? I ask for only a few of the key concepts they learned, as I have found that to be more realistic in initiating change. If you gain insights without action, this book will be only partially useful. However, if you gain insights *and* take action, this book will be much more useful and potentially transformational. When you finish this book, ask yourself the same questions: What did I learn—about myself, about leadership, and about my leadership story? And what am I willing and prepared to do about it?

The Driving Catalyst

What happens to people to make them want to lead—and lead successfully? My daughter would say it was a seed that got planted inside them. Said another way, what's the instigation, the driver, the prompt, or the script change that altered how they acted as a leader? What flipped the switch? Was it some dramatic turning point? Some change of heart or viewpoint, or did they receive some life-changing criticism? Somewhere in their career development something changed, and they found themselves with a new compass.

How often have you heard someone ask, "What drives that guy, anyhow?"

When Paul O'Neill took over as CEO of Alcoa in 1987, he faced a serious leadership wall. Trust at plants was lacking because of equipment safety failures. Unions wanted action, especially because plant managers did not enforce safety rules. What did O'Neill choose as the driver for his leadership of the sprawling Alcoa? Worker safety. He gave his home phone number to workers to call if something was broken or unsafe. Plant managers learned quickly that they could be fired for covering up a safety violation. By the time O'Neill left the company in 2000, trust and quality had improved, and so had revenue. The annual net income was five times higher than in 1987. And he started not with quarterly numbers and stock value but with worker safety.

Nelson Mandela turned his 27 years in prison into a drive for racial reconciliation in South Africa. He had the votes to become president and could have chosen revenge. He did not, and the country was better for it.

Howard Schultz, legendary Starbucks CEO, never forgot how his father had been fired after breaking his leg on a delivery route. The family lost its income and its health care. Schultz's drive was to create a successful company that gave all employees health-care benefits.

I want to help you identify that driver, that seed as my daughter calls it, that dramatic change that can help you write your leadership story. On that basis, we can develop the story's plot in chapter 2, Step 1.

Introducing Bob

But first, let's introduce the subject of our running case study, Bob. Bob works in a large service organization, and he's had several such jobs utilizing his expertise in other firms. Bob is an innovative thinker, a creative person, who, when left to his space, comes up with great ideas. But as I indicated in the introduction, he wants to determine whether he should continue as he is in his profession or take on more duties. Is he ready to be a leader? His anxiety stems from a true dilemma: this ... or that, and is he taking on too much?

"Tim, I've had a great run in my profession. I've worked for many companies. Each gave me wide latitude to create new stuff, and I like that. But I am jumping around a lot. Five employers in the last 15 years. It's taking a toll on my family."

"Why did you leave each company, Bob?" I asked him.

"Well, others were being tapped for bigger projects, so I figured it was time to move on. What's more, each new company was in a different market space, and it seemed like a good way to learn."

"OK, but what I am hearing is this: you want to settle down a little, on the personal level, so what do you want to give up?"

"I guess I have to give up the thrill of my own pet projects and become a team leader. But recently a bunch of my peers and I took a leisurely Friday lunch after I announced that I was leaving the company. Conversation started with questions about the new job and then drifted to projects and promotions at my current firm. I started talking about my projects. "You guys are taking on bigger projects with more admin stuff, but I am off to learn a new business."

"Stop right there, Bob. How did your lunch mates react to that statement?" I asked.

"Well, I asked why they were doing that, giving up their own autonomy and all. But I guess the implication of my question just plopped down right on the table and kind of sat there: why not me? An uneasy silence came over the group. They started, you know, checking their iPhones and fidgeting."

"After the dead air, did anyone say anything more?" I asked.

"One guy smiled kind of weakly and said something about the value of larger teams, something like running a big team develops more winners and innovators, and most companies want that. He added, 'But it takes people who can lead. It's one thing to be a technocrat or expert in your profession, but it's a bigger thing to become a leader of other experts.' Then he said something I have never heard of or thought of before. He said, 'Bob, you have to develop a new profession—leadership. Not just project management. Not just managing a couple of people. Strategic leadership.'

"And then another guy at the table said it more emphatically. He told me that I needed to go after and begin leading big teams where I would set the vision, motivate and develop the team members—*and deliver big results.* He said that for big companies, it's pure economics, like the multiplier effect."

"How did that one hit you, Bob?" I asked.

"Well, the third guy piped up. I could tell he was real uncomfortable, you know, scrunching up his mouth. He said I had the reputation of being a lone ranger, a control freak. The others smiled uneasily at that one. Wow. I had no idea I was perceived that way. I was shocked. It was quite an awakening, like the mirror just got refocused right in front of me."

"So did that casual lunch become a turning point for you?"

"It surely did. Tim, I am realizing something I hadn't thought about before. Expertise is one profession, but eventually you have to apply your individual expertise to the leadership of others—teams, sometimes big teams—to become really, really valuable. I have to stop being a lone ranger. I've got to learn how to lead strategic teams. By being a better leader myself, I will have the potential to get greater results and to have a greater impact on others. That can be a lot of pressure. But I am not sure I can rise to that level of responsibility. Can I become that big a leader? Do I have the right stuff—or should I stick with the path I am on? Can you walk me through your process?"

We will visit with Bob as we walk him, and you, the reader, through each step. It may not be a completely sunny walk, but you will be grateful for the exercise.

CHAPTER II

Understanding and Aligning Your Leadership Story

Your leadership story is complex and dynamic. Since leadership is a journey that involves the past, present, and future, your leadership story evolves. It is the result of numerous factors over time. The good news? Your leadership story has developed and will continue to develop. This suggests that you have the ability to reflect on and learn from the past. It also suggests that you have the ability to shape the future of your leadership story. Doing so will take work and commitment on your part. It also requires that you start with a framework in which to think about your leadership story.

To understand or write a story, as we all learned in literature classes, you have to consider several elements of your story and provide details that will help it to have the desired impact.

But do not misinterpret what I am saying. By putting forth these story elements, I am not encouraging you to fictionalize your life. Rather, you are using them as tools to understand how your story might well vary from how others describe your leadership. You should not have two leadership stories contradicting each other. When that happens, you will be perceived as lacking authenticity. Over time, it will drain the energy and motivation from those you lead. What's more, your true story, your fuller story, goes beyond your surface appearance to your more deeply held values, beliefs, and actions.

What Makes a Good Story?

Every story has several key components: plot, characters, conflict, theme, and setting. Your leadership story is no different. For your leadership story to be authentic, you need to add details and feelings for richness around each element, and you need your perceptions to be aligned with others' perceptions.

Every leadership story must have a plot. *Step 1* focuses on the plot of your leadership story. Within this context, your plot is *why* you do what you do. It focuses on what provides you with a sense of purpose. It is what inspires and motivates you. It clarifies and reinforces your values as a leader. You have to know where you are going, or no one will follow you. This is the starting point for understanding your views of your leadership story. But knowing where you want to go and what drives you is only one part of the equation. You also have to know what is important to others, as this will shape their interpretations of your story.

Stories are filled with characters. You are the central character of your own leadership story. To be effective as a leader, you need to create a connection to the other characters. *Step 2* explores the characters and nature of your relationships in your story. The other characters in your leadership story can serve as champions, or protagonists, or they can be detractors, or antagonists. When you're seeking to understand others' perceptions of your story, the characters are the starting point. You must identify who the key characters of your story are, what their role is, and their perceptions of your story.

No story would be complete without conflict. Conflict reveals the struggle. The struggle in your leadership story can be with people or uncertainty around your plot, tasks, and resources, to name a few examples. With regard to your leadership story, leadership is not just about getting results; it is about how you do so. In *Step 3,* we will expand on the role of conflict in your leadership story.

The theme of a story is the main idea. In your leadership story, the theme comes through in the form of behaviors, skills, and habits. *Step 4* delves into the role of theme in your leadership story. It looks at how you think you are doing in key areas of leadership, as well as how others think you are doing.

Stories take place in a setting. It can be a single setting or a variety of settings. In your leadership story, the setting can play a critical role in shaping your plot, introducing you to characters, and developing your theme. In *Step 5,* we will explore the role of setting in your leadership story. We will examine the elements that allow you to be at your best, as well as how you contribute to others' being at their best.

STEP 1

Define Your Plot

Your plot is the inspiration behind your action. It answers the question of *why* you do what you do. It is the foundation of your leadership story. This is also referred to as your *mission* or *purpose,* and it is likely driven by what you value, or hold important. Understanding your purpose as a leader can have profound impact on you and those around you. Further, what others around you value will have a profound impact on how they interpret your story.

Besides being highly enlightening and personally motivational to those around you, the plot provides clarity around your intent and helps guide your decisions. It can provide inspiration for you and those around you. And that inspiration and energy can be contagious.

Along these lines, your role as a leader is to instill a sense of purpose. Your plot, if well defined and articulated, can also be a source of inspiration for others. On the other hand, if your purpose is not well defined or you don't believe in your purpose, then how can you expect others to believe in it? How can you expect others to be inspired or to follow you?

In addition to reflecting your mission or purpose, your plot is largely driven by your values. Your core values are your fundamental beliefs that drive your performance. I have heard core values referred to as guiding principles. They are at the heart of your leadership story and will drive your identity as a leader. In the activities below, you will have the opportunity to reflect on your core values, or guiding principles.

I typically hear certain questions at this point: Why do I need a personal mission, and what happens if I don't have one? What is the benefit of expressing my personal mission to others? Do I really have to declare what my mission and values are, and how and when do I do so?

John tackled similar questions. He always did well in his job. He had studied business in school, took a job in the finance department of his company, and was progressing in his career. He was personable, he showed initiative, and the quality of his work was always above average. He had four junior employees as direct reports, but he always had an uneasy feeling about his role as a leader. He felt as though he was just going through the motions, and he wasn't even sure if they were the right motions. As a result, the energy of his team was flat—as if they were just going through the motions, too.

By chance, one of his colleagues, Susan, invited him to be a guest speaker at her team meeting. As he sat through the meeting, he observed something he had not experienced in team meetings before. There was a palpable energy in the room. Everyone was listening intently, providing feedback in an open, constructive dialogue. It almost seemed as though they were having fun. He couldn't help but notice that Susan's team was even more upbeat outside of the meetings. So it wasn't just about having fun meetings.

John wanted to know what energized Susan's team so much. A month after observing her team in a variety of work settings, he finally asked her what the trick was for making her meetings so positive. She claimed that there was no trick—they were all working toward the same goal.

Susan explained that she had done three things, shortly after taking over the team, that became the rallying cry or anchor for how the team worked. First, she wrote down what she personally wanted to accomplish as a leader: she wanted to be a leader who provided growth and development opportunities for her team, and who introduced solutions that added value to the business. Second, she wrote down what she thought was important to getting the work done. She wrote down things like fun (not surprisingly), respect, collaboration, and expertise. She explained that she shared these with her team and said, "That is how we will get our work done, and we can all hold each other to it." And third, she set out to learn more about them on a personal level and to hear directly about individuals' interests and goals. She scheduled a meeting with every person on her team. It was a big undertaking and took time over and above the project work she was responsible for.

John thought about what Susan told him. He had never considered this approach before. But he figured, why not give it a try? Writing down the qualities of the leader he wanted to be proved more difficult than he had imagined. He really struggled with it. But after two months and several iterations, he felt that he had something he was comfortable with.

At the next meeting with his team, he explained that he had not given leadership—particularly his own leadership—much attention but that he had been working on it over the last couple of months. He told his team that he wanted to change—to be a better leader, not just for himself but for them—and that he was going to need their help. He unveiled his mission statement and shared his values concerning how the work was going to get done. One of his values was collaboration. So, true to his word, he asked for feedback.

REFLECTIVE QUESTIONS TO THINK ABOUT PLOT

1. What has been most rewarding in your career? Why?
2. What is your quest or challenge as a leader? Where and how do you want to make a difference/have impact?
3. What is important to you as a leader? Why?
4. What inspires and energizes you as a leader?
5. What would you like to accomplish as a leader?

Activities to Build and Refine Your Plot

The first two activities in this section—Define Leadership and What Do You Value?—are adapted from Steve Arneson's book *Bootstrap Leadership: 50 Ways to Break Out, Take Charge and Move Up.*[3] They are so important to the foundation of developing your leadership story that I included them here. The fifth activity—You're on a Mission—is adapted from Jim Loehr's book *The Power of Story: Change Your Story, Change Your Destiny in Business and in Life.*[4] Loehr has a great framework and takes a broader view of story than I do here. Whereas he focuses on your life story, I am focused on understanding and developing your leadership story.

Activity	For Self	Give to Others
Define Leadership	✓	✓
What Do You Value?	✓	✓
Solid Grounds	✓	
Get Excited	✓	
You're on a Mission	✓	

DEFINE LEADERSHIP

There are countless definitions of leadership in textbooks and on the Internet. I am not suggesting that you recite any or all of them, but it is important, as a leader, for you to identify what you believe leadership means. It should be inherently your point of view. You should base it on your personal experience as well as on any books you have read, stories you are familiar with, or insights you have gained from others.

Think about what it means for you to be a leader of other people. What are the expectations that go along with that? What are the skills required to lead effectively? What do you view as the most important aspects of being a leader? Once you have written these ideas down, be sure to revisit them, and be prepared to share them with others.

To be an effective leader means to

You will be giving some of the activities in this book to other people with the aim of initiating a conversation that will help you to better understand how you are perceived by others. The first is to ask select individuals—including direct reports, peers, and your boss—how they think you define leadership. The second is to ask them how they define leadership. It should be a guided conversation. The first approach should be utilized where you are an established leader. It provides insights into how your actions and priorities are being perceived. The second could be used for new or established teams. It provides insights into how your views align with others' and lends itself to establishing a common leadership language among your team.

How do you think I define leadership?

_____

_____

What do you think it means to be an effective leader?

_____

_____

WHAT DO YOU VALUE?

This activity consists of three parts. The first requires a bit of reflection on what you believe as a leader. What fundamentally drives your behaviors and decisions that you are unwilling to compromise? The second part requires gathering observations of how others view what you value as a leader. It will help illustrate what gets rewarded and what is discouraged by you. And the third part involves action.

In order to create a level of accountability and ownership, once you have defined your core values and understand how others perceive those values, you need to communicate them. I recommend starting with your team. Let them know what you value; and where there is misalignment, establish a plan for acting differently.

For this activity, think about what is important to you about leading other people. How do you value interpersonal interaction? What personality characteristics or traits do you hold in high regard? Is there anything about working with a team that you hold important? Other work processes? Outcomes? Does anything outside of work factor into your values?

It may help to think about a situation in which you were faced with a difficult decision or some other challenge you needed to work through. How you made your decision, whether or not you were aware of it, may have been driven largely by your core values. Remember, these are truly yours—what you hold as imperative and are unwilling to compromise or waver about. Most people have 5 to 10 core values, although you can have more or less.

As a leader, I value...

_____

_____

What do I reward or recognize?   What do I discourage?

_____   _____

_____   _____

_____   _____

_____   _____

Where there is a lack of alignment, what will I do differently?

_____

_____

SOLID GROUND

As a leader, you will likely be required to compromise on some issues. You will have to take a stand or have a position about various subjects. You should have a clear understanding of those things on which you are unwilling to compromise. That is a natural part of leadership. And it is your job as leader to build the best culture you can—one that is productive, collaborative, flexible, and fair, and delivers results that matter.

As part of this, you may find a few areas in which you are unwilling to compromise. These usually center on your core values. The likelihood is that you can act out of your core values in a variety of ways without having to compromise them. For this activity, write down those few areas that are anchors to your leadership story—that you are unwilling to compromise on.

As an example, you may value collaboration and teamwork. If you are working on a project that is not exhibiting the level of teamwork you would like, you might say something. But you could likely adapt to the situation without compromising your values. On the other hand, if you see individuals taking credit for work that isn't theirs, or they are otherwise not giving credit for work done as a group, you might find that unacceptable and beyond compromise.

Take a look back at your core values as a starting point and write down (a) those critical areas that you hold sacred, (b) what specifically you will do to reinforce the positive aspects of those behaviors, and (c) how you would handle a breach of those behaviors.

Critical Behavior	Proactive Action	Reaction
_____	_____	_____
_____	_____	_____
_____	_____	_____

GET EXCITED

I recently met somebody for the first time at a conference. We got into a brief conversation about who we were, what we did, and how we had arrived at this point in our careers. As we each took turns discussing our background (or story), I noticed two very interesting points. As we each told our story, we chose to highlight certain aspects and, speaking for myself, left out a considerable amount. I wondered why I chose to highlight what I did. Clearly, when meeting someone for the first time, you don't want to give every last detail of your story. How do you determine what you would like to share about yourself? The second interesting observation was that we each expressed enthusiasm around certain aspects of our story. I had never thought about that before. I should point out that we asked each other questions such as "What did you do there?" "Why did you leave that job?" "What did you love (or not) about that job? About your current job?"

Here is your chance to think about what you're enthusiastic about. For this activity, think back to your journey thus far. Write a brief story of what got you to this point. Imagine that you are telling someone about your path to where you are today. What do you highlight? What do you get excited about? List what inspires and motivates you about your work and being a leader. When it comes to your list, more specificity will allow you to make a personal connection with your own story. Also, focusing on the positives can generate some excitement and possible clarity around what energizes you.

YOU'RE ON A MISSION

Early in my career, I always wondered why I had a slightly uneasy feeling about it. I was challenged. I was learning a lot. I was contributing in the field I had prepared for. Or so I thought.

It wasn't until many years into my career that I took the time to think about what I truly loved to do at work. The work I had been doing was not far off from my true mission, which may or may not have helped because I did not feel so disoriented about my work that I had to change. I was just a little uneasy about my career. I was doing work I thought I was supposed to do, based on my education, my experience, and what other people thought I should do. It was not what I truly wanted to do.

I had no personal leadership mission statement and had never given it a thought. My leadership story and career were on cruise control. It was not until I was up for a promotion—which I thought I wanted because I should be moving up in my career—that I realized it was not what I wanted at all. The promotion would have taken me further away from the work that energized me the most. I asked myself, "What is it that I really want to do?" Sometimes, by looking at what you don't want to do, you can begin to narrow down what you do want to do.

I took the time to write my personal leadership mission statement. It has gone through a couple of iterations, but I have found it to be fairly durable. Your personal leadership mission statement can be powerful for you and for others. It can provide clarity of purpose and direct your energy. It can motivate and inspire others as well.

As luck would have it, I was able to try out some projects in my then-current role that were much closer to my interest. I think the saying is "Like a duck to water." My ideas expanded, as did my energy. Having that clarity allowed me to make the decision to do more of the work that inspired and motivated me and others. And do you know what? My energy and enthusiasm grew and became contagious.

Make no mistake, the change was risky. I realized that I could further clarify my mission statement with more experience and insights. And I am always fine-tuning how I enact my mission.

Write your personal leadership mission statement. This should not be a summary of the work you do today; rather, it should be an aspirational statement that gets you excited to lead people and do your work. It is a combination of looking back at what has inspired you in the past and looking forward at what you will strive to be as a leader. Consider the following questions:

- What do you want to accomplish as a leader above all else?
- What are you dedicated to as a leader?
- Where do you bring the greatest value?
- What provides you with the greatest sense of satisfaction as a leader?
- How do you want to be remembered as a leader?
- What is the leadership legacy you want to leave?
- What impact do you want to have on others?

Note: Effective mission statements are straightforward, one to three sentences max. Your mission should have two parts. The first part should focus on the contribution you want to make: what you want to accomplish and for whom. You should include a verb and write it in the present tense. The second part of your mission statement should convey the purpose behind why you lead. What impact will you have on the audience? Think in terms of results, impact, and legacy.

Personal mission statements can be refined over time, but you have to start somewhere.

My personal mission is to...

Quick Tips

To Build and Refine Your Plot

1. You must know what you believe in and where you want to go as a leader in order for others to be inspired to follow.

2. Identify what inspires and energizes you about your work.

3. Sharing your point of view with others will hold you accountable.

Bob Ponders His Plot

Our colleague Bob has been low-key since that fateful lunch. Low-key at best, blown away at worst.

"Tim, this plot thing. I know what a story plot is. Everyone does. But I've had a good career, and my résumé says that. I hold certification in my field. There. Is your leadership story just a longer version of your elevator speech?"

"A story has to be interesting, Bob. It contains facts, yes, but it also contains qualitative things that speak to emotions—yours and those of the folks around you," I told him. "It has to have elements that people notice, grab on to, and ask you about."

"Give me some color and flavor here," Bob asked somewhat impatiently.

"OK, what is more fun—managing project after project, small tactical projects, all done well, I am sure? Or a big game-changing project? Maybe "project" is too limited a term. Which success would make for a better leadership story, Bob? And who wouldn't want to be led by a game-changing leader on a significant strategic effort?

Steve Jobs didn't lead projects. Steve Jobs reinvented entire aspects of our lives. And he led energized people. He was a tough, demanding boss, but look what he did, and look at the talent he developed. Think of it this way: Managing is about spreadsheets. We're not talking project management here. Leadership is about the potential for evolution. That takes vision and the ability to foster followership. Inspired leadership involves inspired followership. So your leadership story has to have a plot that is distinctive. It's not just numbers; it's emotions."

"Good examples, Tim. But I'm not a crusader or revolutionary. I haven't invented anything yet."

"But you have a view of how your profession operates and perhaps could operate differently. Maybe you have a different focal point."

"Well, sure, I do, but it never occurred to me that point of view was something about leadership."

"Your lunch mates that day may agree. What drives your point of view, and how did you reach it? What was the turning point, or what happened?

What hit you? And why wouldn't you want to induct others, so to speak, into the same tour de force?"

STEP 2

Identify and Build Strong Relationships with Your Key Characters

As a leader, you need to understand the role of characters in your story, the role of perceptions, who your protagonists and antagonists are, and the impact you have on others and others on you. Why should you care about some abstraction called characters? Because they are real and concrete and all around you. What's more, you are one of the main characters, but not the only one.

This aspect of your leadership story is about both the quality and quantity of your relationships. It is also important that you build strong relationships with the characters around you, learn from them, and express your gratitude.

As a leader, you may be called upon to be heroic. You may need to make difficult decisions and have difficult conversations, to believe in others when they do not believe in themselves, to inspire and motivate, and to help people achieve greatness and attain their fullest potential. But *how* you do this makes a difference. When it comes to your personal leadership story, who are your heroes? And to whom are you a hero?

Leadership is not about telling people what to do or having them adjust to your style. Leadership is about people. It requires a great deal of awareness of self and others. It requires emotional intelligence. Emotional intelligence refers to your ability to recognize and consider your emotions and feelings as well as the feelings of others. The concept was popularized by Daniel Goleman in his book *Emotional Intelligence: Why It Can Matter More Than IQ.*[5] This may be more important than ever for leaders in our action-oriented, technology-based culture.

Sure, you can probably get the job done with little attention to the characters—who they are or what they need. But how effective will it be? And could it have been a little better if you had included a focus on the characters? Understanding the characters is about relationships—whom you have them with and how you cultivate them. You are the main character in your leadership story, but others play an important role in your leadership story as well. It is profoundly difficult to be a leader if no one around you—the characters—wants to be led by you.

Whether through action or inaction, awareness or lack of awareness, you own your leadership story. Because of the role of characters, the challenge here is that your story can never truly be self-authored. Leaders get better or worse as judged by those around them. You may well be the primary author of *your* leadership story, but transformational leadership also lives in the observations, perceptions, and interpretations of others. For example, what you view as providing autonomy may be viewed by others as being disengaged.

Stephanie was hired right out of graduate school, where she was one of the top students in her graduating class. She was given leadership responsibility right away, and she wanted to make a great first impression. She often worked into the evening to ensure that her work exceeded everyone's expectations. Although she had the obligatory one-to-one meetings with members of her team, her primary focus was on getting the work done. During office hours, her door was often closed as she worked on a variety of projects. She usually ate lunch in her office and rarely said more than "Good morning" to her peers and colleagues. When it came time for the annual organizational climate survey, she received some of the lowest scores. Stephanie was getting the task done well without any consideration of the people she worked with.

The single most important thing you can do toward becoming the author of your leadership story is to understand how others perceive your leadership. You may think you are showing up one way only to find that it is not the case.

For example, you may think you are coming across as supportive and involved in the details, when you are being perceived as a micromanager who doesn't trust his employees. You should consider the designated activities in this book as starting points to involve others in understanding your leadership story. You are best served if you can gather perceptions anonymously to encourage candor.

Another useful tool to facilitate this process is a leadership 360. We will have more on 360 assessments in "Step 4: Develop Your Theme." However, for the purposes of understanding others' perceptions of you, I would encourage you to do a 360 assessment if (a) you have never done one before, (b) it has been more than two years since you did one, or (c) you have been in your role for over one year. Consider making this important pulse check part of your routine and ongoing development.

There is a saying that you should not judge a book by its cover. In other words, one needs to take the time and effort to understand what exists beyond the surface. And yet, in terms of others' perceptions, I have seen human nature in action here. Even in instances when people in the workplace *heard* a detail about you but did not *experience* it for themselves, they are inclined to carry that as part of your leadership story. In fact, it is typical that whatever that aspect of your story is, they will likely look for additional data to validate what they have heard. And this is where others' perceptions can be quite powerful: they are becoming the authors of your leadership story, and you may not even be aware of it. This can work for or against you, depending on what element of your story people have heard. For the greatest impact, your objective should be to ensure that others' perception of your leadership story is aligned with your reality.

Your own perceptions of yourself can also play a critical role in your leadership story. Quite simply, do you believe in yourself as a leader? Why or why not? What has happened to make you think that way? What has shaped your mind-set? How might you navigate any uncertainty that you have? The objective is not to operate in a delusional state about your capabilities and think that you can accomplish things that you cannot. The intent is to truly know your capabilities and believe in them. And where there is uncertainty, seek the advice and guidance of others.

When it comes to your leadership story, several debatable questions center on the characters. For example, I am often asked, "Do you have to be liked to be an effective leader?" "Do you have to be authentic to be an effective leader?" "Do you have to be trusted to be an effective leader?" Unequivocally, no. There are many examples throughout history of leaders who were not necessarily well liked, authentic, or trusted. Fear may be an effective approach to get results, but does it contribute to effective leadership?

Think about the human side of leadership rather than the task side. Remember that the portion of your leadership story dealing with character is about relationships. If the only purpose were to get results, you would not need to consider things like trust, authenticity, and likability. However, if your focus includes *how* you get the work done, establishing relationships, and inspiring others, then you do need to consider them. Characteristics like trust, authenticity, and likability come into play with regard to being respected, relating to others or affinity, and making an emotional connection.

A great leadership tactic to increase involvement and establish stronger connections with your characters is to ask the simple question "What do you think?" This tip comes directly from J.W. "Bill" Marriott Jr.'s book *Without Reservations.*[6] Asking this shows that you care and are open to considering others' suggestions that might yield interesting insights you had not considered. As a leader, you still need to make the decisions, and they may or may not be in line with what others suggested. The key is that you engage others in the process.

As with any story, protagonists and antagonists will be part of your leadership story. The protagonists are your champions. More often, these are established leaders within the organization who act as your credibility substitutes. They vouch for you when you're not there. Protagonists don't often think you are perfect, but they do believe in you and your potential. They have your interests in mind and look for challenging opportunities for you. They want to see you grow, develop, and succeed. I have found that protagonists often work behind the scenes supporting other leaders.

Why would anyone want to be your protagonist? And how do you get more protagonists in your leadership story? Unfortunately, there is not a standard formula. However, I have seen some consistent circumstances where people are more likely to be your champion. First, from a process standpoint, it is uncommon for an individual to ask someone to be his or her champion or protagonist. Over the years, I have identified simple factors that prompt people to willingly become one's champion or protagonist: capability, effort, willingness to learn, relating well to others or affinity, likability, and even humility. It usually takes a combination of several of these characteristics. Protagonists implicitly want to know (a) whether you have what it takes to succeed, (b) whether they like you enough to want you to succeed, and (c) whether you will make them (the champion) and the organization look good.

Unfortunately, nearly every story has at least one antagonist. You might be asking, "Gee, how do I spot the antagonist if I am busy working?" The antagonist is a detractor. People can show up as antagonists in your leadership story for any number of reasons. They can be subordinates, peers, clients, competitors for a promotion, or supervisors. They can be antagonists based on motivations or perceptions, whether accurate or not. In terms of motivation, people may not want to see you succeed because they believe that success is a zero-sum game: if you succeed, they don't. Or their success is altered or delayed. They may not want you to succeed because they don't like you. Perhaps you gave someone a poor performance rating. Whether it was deserved or not, if the person doesn't think it was deserved, she may have it out for you. These are simple examples, and it is difficult to judge why someone would be your antagonist. What is important, though, is that you be aware of who might be an antagonist, and then you can seek to understand why.

You can even be the antagonist in your own leadership story. This can occur if, for example, you don't believe in yourself, give little effort, don't learn and grow, don't honor commitments, are disrespectful to others, or do not do what you say you will do.

In *The Extraordinary Leader: Turning Good Managers into Great Leaders,* authors John Zenger and Joseph Folkman refer to these behaviors as "fatal flaws."[7] I have also seen them referred to as "derailers." It is important that you become aware if you have any fatal flaws and then take action to change or minimize them. Note that if you have had fatal flaws that were unchecked for some time, your leadership story may have been adversely affected all that time. Depending on who has been involved, you may need to acknowledge the behavior publicly, apologize to the individual(s) affected, and demonstrate that you will change.

So how do you deal with antagonists in your leadership story? Again, since motivations, experiences, perceptions, and situations can be so varied, there is not a single magic formula. But some things can help mitigate antagonists and their influence. It begins with self-awareness. You need to be aware of how you treat other people and their needs, and of the impact that may have. That sounds a lot like having high emotional intelligence, and it is true. Also helpful: show effort, demonstrate fairness, don't try to get ahead at others' expense, don't talk behind people's backs, and set clear expectations.

And even if you live by the Golden Rule—to treat others the way you would want to be treated—that still may not be enough to avoid having an antagonist. I'm not trying to make you paranoid and think that antagonists are out there lurking in the shadows. I'm not even suggesting that everyone has antagonists in their story. But what I would point out is that most of the people I have worked with were surprised to find out that they had an antagonist. You might even say that they were caught off guard.

If you do come across an antagonist, it will be important for you to devote some time to repairing that relationship and understanding the person's motivation. We discuss this further in "Step 3: Prepare for Conflict," but it is important that this not be left unchecked. Antagonists can do irreparable harm to your leadership story.

REFLECTIVE QUESTIONS TO THINK ABOUT YOUR CHARACTERS

1. With whom are your key relationships at work? Who impacts your ability to do your best work, and how do you impact others' ability to do their best work?
2. How can you build more supporters and champions of your leadership story than detractors?

3. What role do you play in your leadership story? Others? (Hero, villain, etc.) Why?
4. Who are your trusted advisors?
5. How would others describe you as a leader? How well is your leadership story aligned with others' interpretation of your leadership story?

Activities to Identify and Build Strong Relationships with Your Characters

Activity	For Self	Give to Others
Keys to Unlocking Connections	✓	✓
Common Ground	✓	
Monitor the Emotional Bank Account	✓	✓
Build Mentor Circles	✓	
Common Ground	✓	
Thank You!	✓	

KEYS TO UNLOCKING CONNECTIONS

You may have heard the saying "Whom you know is more important than what you know." One thing is for sure: leadership is a relationship business. Both the quality and the quantity of relationships are important aspects of your leadership story. And, as discussed previously, alignment matters.

Navigating the organizational waters and ensuring a broad audience for your leadership story requires you to have a good number of positive relationships. I am not suggesting that you have to like or get along with everyone. However, you need to be both aware of the status of your relationships (i.e., protagonist or antagonist) and strategic with key relationships.

For this activity, make a list of your protagonists/champions and antagonists/detractors, in order of importance. You can list those people who are actually your champion or those whose support is important to you. Note why each is an important relationship for you, and then write down what you need to do to maintain or improve his or her status toward being a protagonist. This should provide insights into which relationships you need to foster.

Protagonist

Person	Importance	Action
_____	_____	_____
_____	_____	_____
_____	_____	_____

Antagonist

Person	Importance	Action
_____	_____	_____
_____	_____	_____
_____	_____	_____

Since it is unlikely that someone would identify you outright as his or her antagonist, the variation of this activity for others is to understand the extent to which you support others. I recommend engaging a broader audience than you identified above for this activity. Include all of your direct reports, a breadth of peers from across the organization, and your boss. Ask them to rate on a scale of 1 to 10 (10 being high) how supportive you are to them personally or their mission. Anything below an 8—some would say 10—requires your attention. Ask them how you could support them better.

COMMON GROUND

This activity is adapted from Alan Gregerman's book *The Necessity of Strangers.*[8] As a follow-on to the activity above, for the key relationships you listed—with both protagonists and antagonists—your job over the next 30 days is to identify at least five non-work-related things you have in common with each person. Finding common ground allows you to establish stronger relationships, work toward better results, inspire problem solving, provide better ideas, and reinforce your leadership story. Give yourself five points for each person with whom you identify some common ground.

Person	Common Ground
_____	_____
_____	_____
_____	_____
_____	_____
_____	_____
_____	_____
_____	_____

MONITOR THE EMOTIONAL BANK ACCOUNT

The notion of an emotional bank account gained wide attention by being featured in Stephen Covey's book *The 7 Habits of Highly Effective People.*[9] It is centered on trust and refers to the deposits and withdrawals you may make with each of your relationships. Deposits are the result of building trust based on being empathetic, paying attention to all aspects of the relationship, honoring commitments, recognizing and apologizing in instances where you might have made a withdrawal, clarifying expectations, and demonstrating respect. Withdrawals are the opposite. They are based on something you have done to harm the relationship or trust. A saying that comes to mind concerning trust and relationships is "It takes 99 acts to build trust but only one to tear it down." So you can imagine that your objective is to make far more deposits in your emotional bank account than withdrawals because a single withdrawal can have lasting effects on a relationship and on your leadership story.

Your emotional bank account exists with each individual. It is not transferable. And it is constantly evolving. However, when it comes to your leadership story, you may be given a "line of credit" based on your leadership story—perhaps based on how you are known to treat other people. Deposits and withdrawals can be small, or they can be big.

Into the following form, copy the names from the lists of protagonists and antagonists you made earlier. Note next to each name whether you have a surplus (+) or deficit (−) with each individual, and note when you made a deposit or withdrawal. What did you do in each case? In the case of withdrawals, you need to recognize them and possibly make an apology.

Relationship (with + or −)	Deposit	Withdrawal
_____	_____	_____
_____	_____	_____
_____	_____	_____
_____	_____	_____
_____	_____	_____

This activity should be given to others as well. You may think you are in great standing with many people but then find that you have made some withdrawals that you were not aware of. For the relationships you listed above, provide those people with an imaginary 100 coins that they can allocate to your relationship. Explain that 100 is completely strong and zero is the weakest. Ask them to allocate the coins based on how strong they perceive the relationship. Anything less than 100 indicates that you have made a withdrawal at some point. You may ask them where withdrawals have been made and what could be done to fully replenish the bank account.

BUILD MENTOR CIRCLES

Leadership is pretty heady stuff. It is complex. You will likely be faced with very difficult decisions for which you have limited data or personal experience. You are not alone—or at least you shouldn't be. While self-reflection is a great tool and one that should be exercised often, you also need trusted advisors you can call on as necessary.

The mentor circles that I am most familiar with involve bringing in a single leader to mentor a small group of people on multiple occasions over some period of time. You can bring in the same mentor multiple times or rotate among multiple mentors. It is important to provide some structure.

For this activity, we are going to modify the process to the advantage of your leadership story. Rather than finding a single leader, your job is to identify several leaders (perhaps three to five) who can provide mentoring and guidance and be trusted advisers to you. A couple of rules/tips for this activity:

- You need to be realistic in your aims. For example, if you are just beginning your journey as a leader, it may not be realistic to have the CEO as part of your mentor circle.
- Consider people inside and outside of your current organization. And also consider people from different backgrounds, perspectives, and possibly industries.
- Keep in mind your existing relationships with the individuals. If you do not know them, they will be less likely to offer support and guidance, and the support they do offer may not be as valuable or relevant.
- Consider access. Do you have ready access to the individual?
- You don't need to identify all of the people in your mentor circle at this moment—it can and should evolve.
- To the extent possible, this should be a two-way relationship; you need to focus on being a good listener and on opportunities to contribute ideas and insights about challenges your mentors are facing.

- Provide some clarity to the individuals for your request. What are you asking for? Why?
- Once the relationship and expectations are agreed upon, avoid too much structure. For example, I have seen standing, recurring meetings fail because they were forced. What seems to work well is to establish some flexibility for an occasional discussion as needed. Also recommended: Don't tax the generosity of the mentors, and express your thanks for their input.

THANK YOU!

Gratitude and appreciation are given far too rarely in leadership and in life. In fact, throughout my career I have observed leaders who sought to take credit rather than to give it. As the saying goes, "Success has many fathers, but failure is an orphan."

Let's face it, we have been influenced by any number of people throughout our career. And hopefully we have influenced many as well. But this activity is about gratitude and appreciation for the people (aka characters) who have had a positive impact on your life. These are the people who have shown you the way and what it means to be a great leader. I have been fortunate to encounter several influential leaders. Some I've stayed in touch with and others I have not. But the impact of all of them has been profound.

Who has had the greatest influence on your leadership? This is a great activity, and you should consider its applicability beyond leadership. Every day for a week, take one uninterrupted minute and make a list of the people who have had the greatest positive influence on your life. Then, next to each name, note what you are grateful to the person for. It does not have to be a boss; it could be a peer or colleague, a direct report, or someone outside of work.

Who has been most influential? Who has shaped you as a leader? What have they taught you about leadership (or possibly life)? In your list, include attributes you learned from them. Do you have a short example or story of how or when you learned a particular characteristic or skill from them? As an added bonus, if possible, contact the individuals to let them know the impact they have had on you and what you learned from them, and thank them.

Bob Tackles His Characters

I pushed Bob a little more on his colleagues at work. "Why were they hesitant to approach you before that farewell lunch? You got along with them pretty well, didn't you?" I asked.

"Well, we never had any arguments. Certainly we discussed the pros and cons of different approaches to our projects."

"When you laid your opinion on the table those times, how did the conversations proceed?" I pressed.

"The conversations didn't go much further," he replied.

Then I asked Bob a tougher question: "How was your exit interview with your boss?"

"It was OK, I guess," he said nervously. "We always got along fine, good reviews, no major disagreements ... and he wished me well."

"Didn't he have any parting advice?" I asked. "After all, you were hours from being out the door."

"Yeah, he said he hoped I took on some bigger projects, more strategic projects, at my next company; and maybe those big-picture leadership successes might be valuable back here someday, he said with a friendly smile."

Do you think Bob has protagonists and antagonists? He may have had one protagonist, his boss, or he wouldn't have lasted. But can you imagine in which category his lunch mates fit? Hard to say. Maybe a little of both. But it took a farewell lunch to get it out of them. If no one cares enough to give you feedback, you are in trouble as a leader.

Sometimes it is easy to become caught in a pattern of action or to set ourselves on cruise control. Relationships take time and effort to cultivate. Had Bob taken the time to get to know any of his lunch mates or even his boss at a deeper level, he would have enabled them to be more comfortable—better yet, *more collegial*—with him. He might have gained significant insight into how building stronger, welcoming, and more collaborative relationships could help him to become a better leader. In the end, though, no one had cared enough one way or the other to say something to him. Bob was Bob, and Bob did well at cranking out projects. He did what he was supposed to do. He got stuff done, while others were more into bigger stuff. It wasn't worth it to them to speak up until Bob was safely out the door. And what kind of leadership story did he leave behind? How will he be remembered at his former peers' next casual Friday lunch?

How much better for Bob's career, and for his longevity at the company, would it have been if he had done the exercises in this step and spent time on the reflective questions and activities?

Quick Tips

To Establish Strong Characters
1. You can learn a lot from both good and bad leaders. Ask yourself

what you would do the same as or differently than leaders you know have done.

2. Proactively build positive relationships and express gratitude.

3. Identify and seek input and guidance from trusted advisors.

STEP 3

Prepare for Conflict

Conflict happens. And it would be hard to imagine a story without any conflict. The initial impression of conflict is that it is a struggle. When we read or watch stories, sometimes it is that struggle that creates a sense of adventure and excitement. It often draws us in. Even in our own lives, looking back on conflict can give us a sense of excitement or pride—pride that we overcame the challenge.

Two sayings come to mind with regard to conflict. The first is that conflict does not build character; conflict reveals it. In other words, how you react or respond to conflict says a lot about you. Do you let it consume you? Do you take out your anxieties on others? Or do you go with the flow? What is your mind-set and approach when it comes to conflict, struggle, and adversity?

The second saying is that it is about the journey, not the destination. You are certain to run into challenges, obstacles, and conflict along the way. In many cases, they will be unexpected. How are you prepared to deal with such conflict? If conflict does happen, what can you learn from it? And how can you be better prepared for any unanticipated future challenges?

Conflict varies in degree and effect. As a leader, you can experience a range from small conflicts or setbacks all the way through larger, more critical conflicts. Additionally, there are multiple types of conflict. On the negative side, you can experience interpersonal conflict or conflict with tasks. You may also experience internal conflict, where you struggle deeply with who you are as a leader. You will have opportunities to explore each type of struggle later in this step.

Interpersonal conflict is between you and another individual or multiple individuals. It is often based on a fundamental difference in opinion, philosophy, personality, or motivation. For example, suppose you have two peers who are both in line for a single promotion. Inherently, that may create conflict of interest; shape their motivations; or affect how they act toward one another (e.g., competitive versus collaborative), as in taking and giving credit, and, most important, in articulating each other's leadership story. In this case, how each handles the conflict is critical to the long-term relationship. As a leader, you have to help ensure that neither individual permanently damages the relationship. This may require considerable patience and communication.

Conflict with tasks may be based on resources or skills. For example, do you have the skills or resources to get a particular task done? Is the timeline feasible or not? This task-focused conflict will have a direct impact on your leadership story. How do you articulate the challenge? Do you bring solutions to bear or merely identify the problems? Do you have a can-do attitude or a can't-do one? This is another place where adversity does not just build your leadership story but reveals it.

Not all conflict is negative. Conflict can sometimes be the source of great ideas. In fact, if you are a leader putting together a team, you will be better served by identifying team members with opposing viewpoints than by assembling a group of like-minded individuals. Although the process in this case can be challenging at times, the team's output is likely to be better and more innovative.

The objective here is for you to build your awareness about the sources of conflict and how you respond to conflict as a leader. It requires awareness about the situations that cause conflict, your preferred or comfortable response, and the impact that your response has on others around you. For some, this may require a shift in mind-set. For example, when you are faced with conflict, does your inner voice or mind-set position you as the hero? The victim? An impostor or fraud? Do you have a bring-it-on mentality or an it'll-never-work mentality? Do you believe in yourself and feel that you have the ability to prevail over the conflict? I tell my kids, if you believe that you can't do something, then that's probably going to be true.

You want to build this conflict-management capability—and your mind-set—just as you would build a muscle. Start with small wins. If you have never been a leader before, lead a portion of a meeting or project. Ask for some guidance initially, but be open to figuring it out for yourself. And most important, give yourself a grade and ask others for feedback. I find that most leaders who have a negative mind-set have tried or been asked to try doing things that were more than a stretch, have not been given proper guidance or resources, or have not received feedback along the way or at the end. Such events should be viewed as a prescriptive or as a guide for future actions.

I mentioned earlier the issue of feeling like an impostor. Sometimes leaders have an inward struggle with who they are as a leader even though they are in a leadership position. A common example is what I call the *impostor phenomenon,* in which some leaders fear, perhaps unconsciously, that they might be exposed as a leadership impostor. Now that is a big conflict issue in any leadership story.

Experience is a great aid for dealing with conflict or adversity. The more experience you have, the more comfortable and confident you are with conflict. You also have a wider lens with which to understand the various solutions available. Since you can't create experience on the spot, a surrogate is your mentor circle. If you have the luxury of time in responding to a particular situation, how would the individuals in your circle handle it? What advice can they share? It is of course up to you whether you take the advice, but having multiple perspectives outside of your own will allow you to broaden your thinking.

Understanding and preparing for conflict has a lot to do with self-awareness. What bothers you or causes you conflict? And how do you feel about it? You may think that sounds too touchy-feely, but frankly a lack of self-awareness will leave you unprepared. It may cause you to react in unproductive ways that damage relationships and ultimately your leadership story.

REFLECTIVE QUESTIONS TO THINK ABOUT CONFLICT

1. What have been recurring causes of conflict for you as a leader (e.g., types of tasks, people, situations)?
2. What is your role in conflict?
3. How do you typically react to, respond to, or handle conflict? How resilient are you? What would others say about how you handle conflict?
4. What is your approach, outlet, or mechanism for processing conflict constructively?
5. How do you resolve conflict? What impact does this have on your relationships? Your ability to get the job done?

Peggy was always skeptical of her ability to lead others. Her supervisors believed in her abilities, so she continued to get increasing leadership responsibilities. Little did anyone know that each additional leadership responsibility prompted a new set of doubts and fears in her about her ability to be an effective leader. She felt as though the curtain was going to be pulled back at any time and she would be found out as a fraud.

One day, Peggy ran into a former boss, Kristine, whom she admired as a great leader. Peggy casually mentioned that she didn't know if she wanted to be a leader anymore. She missed being more of an individual contributor as a technical expert. But she also felt that there was no going back.

Kristine wanted to know more and invited her to lunch the following week. They spent the whole lunch discussing why Peggy felt this way despite having a positive track record and reputation as a leader. It took several conversations for Peggy to realize that no leader is perfect, and she eventually came to look at the positive impact she was having on the team, how she engaged her team, and the positive results. Over time, she shifted her perspective from self-doubt to one of continuous self-development. Peggy learned how to handle the leadership conflict she had had with herself.

Activities to Be Ready for Conflict

Conflict can take many shapes and be minor or major. As with the other aspects of your leadership story, developing your awareness of what causes conflict and how you react to it is an important step in enabling you to handle conflict in the future. It can be challenging because our brains are wired for fight or flight, and neither of those approaches may be suitable for your leadership story. The activities described below provide ways for you to reflect on how you currently handle conflict, as well as to prepare for how you would like to handle it in the future. The first three activities were adapted from an eHow article by Carrie Perles titled "Conflict Management Training Activities."[10]

Activity	For Self	Give to Others
The I's Have It	✓	
What's Happening?	✓	
Learn from the Past, Commit to the Future	✓	✓
What It Takes	✓	✓
The Heart of Innovation	✓	

THE I'S HAVE IT

Conflict is often based on differences of opinion and perspective among multiple people. Too often, we strive to pull others over to our side. There is certainly a time and a place for that. On the other hand, empathy, or putting yourself in others' shoes, is often the last thing on our mind during a conflict. This activity is about shifting to a more empathetic mind-set.

The activity highlights conflict between two individuals. It tends to yield the best results when both parties recognize that conflict exists and are willing and open to resolving it. However, you can conduct it as an individual activity to help you build a mind-set of empathy. For this activity, your job is to reframe everything around the conflict from "you" to "I."

"You" messages can come off as condescending or negative, and they can be ineffective. For example, instead of statements such as "You should..." or "Why did you...," reframe the statement so that it relates to your own feelings. For example, you might say, "I feel X when you..."

When you complete the activity as an individual exercise, you will begin to notice a greater self-awareness about sources of conflict and how you feel about them. That is the pathway to being better prepared for action. It also allows you to better respond to future conflict rather than reacting to it.

WHAT'S HAPPENING?

You can learn a lot from stories—not just your own (and others') leadership stories, but also current events and history. Examining news stories gives you an opportunity to think about how you would handle conflict.

For this activity, make a list of current events involving a conflict between two or more individuals or groups. Make a note about how each side attempted to solve it, as well as how effectively those methods worked. Pay particular attention to your reaction to the conflict, as it may indicate insights about your values. For the second part of the activity, consider how your observations of the way the conflict played out might influence your ability to handle conflict effectively.

Event Summary	Approach	Effectiveness
_____	_____	_____
_____	_____	_____
_____	_____	_____

How is the approach taken from the current event applicable to the ways you might handle conflict?

_____

LEARN FROM THE PAST, COMMIT TO THE FUTURE

Struggles are an inherent part of stories as well as leadership. It is not a matter of *if* you will experience conflict as a leader, it is a matter of *when* and what you will do to prepare for it and learn from it.

There are three parts to this activity. For part one, first think about and list the last three times you had a personal conflict, something unexpectedly came up, or you worked on a difficult task or project. Be as specific as possible. Consider not only what the situation was but also what it was about the situation that troubled you.

Next, make a note of how you reacted to it. What were your nonverbal and verbal reactions? How did the conflict make you feel?

To close out the first part of the activity, write down what you did. How did you interact with or treat people (e.g., active, passive; proactively address, ignore)? How did you handle the task (e.g., try again, enlist others, give up; take responsibility, defer)?

Situation: Thing That Troubled Me	Reaction: How I Felt	Action: What I Did
_____	_____	_____
_____	_____	_____
_____	_____	_____

For the second part of the activity, ask multiple individuals to identify a situation in which you faced conflict, grade you on how you responded, and note the impact (high, medium, or low) that your response had on them or others. Their comments may reveal ways in which you are not aware of situations, your response, or the impact of your response.

Situation	Reaction Grade	Impact
_____	_____	_____
_____	_____	_____
_____	_____	_____

What does this say about your inner voice, mind-set, and self-awareness with regard to conflict? For the third part of the activity, make a commitment to yourself regarding how you wish to handle conflict the next time it arises. What would you do the same or differently if a similar situation presented itself? Keep in mind, this takes self-awareness, and it takes practice. Allow yourself time to develop this skill just as you would a muscle. You may not get it perfectly the next time conflict arises, but you will move toward a reaction that better supports your desired leadership story. And as an added benefit, you will be on your way to building stronger relationships.

Commitment

The next time I am faced with a similar conflict in the future, I will...

_____

WHAT IT TAKES

In order for you to manage conflict in a way that is complementary to your leadership story, you have to better understand the skills required for conflict management and where you stand relative to those skills, and you need a plan of action to continue to develop your conflict-management skills. The greater your self-awareness and the more planning you do, the more likely it is that there will be a training effect and you will respond to, rather than react to, conflict.

For the first step, write down the skills necessary to manage conflict in your organization. If you are uncertain what those skills are, I encourage you to take one of two approaches. First, over a short period of time—no more than a month—observe how different points of view are expressed in meetings and any other interpersonal interactions. Alternatively, you might check any competency models your organization has and look for the behavioral indicators for conflict management, collaboration, communication, or a related skill. Keep in mind that the latter approach states the ideal and may not represent how conflict is actually addressed within the organization. It is important for you to understand how conflict works in *your* organization. However, if neither of the above is available or yields useful results, another option is to research generic conflict-management skills.

Next, rate yourself on a scale of 1 to 5 (1 being low), relative to those skills. For anything that you rate below a 4, you should have a specific development plan for how you are going to improve that skill. For anything rated a 4 or a 5, you may want to note what you need to do to maintain that capability and possibly to teach it to others.

This activity lends itself nicely to validation from others. Provide them with the same worksheet below. Ask them to identify the skills necessary for conflict management; it will show whether you are aligned in those observations. Ask them to rate how you do with those skills, and get their input for what you could do better.

Conflict Skill	Rating	Action
_____	_____	_____
_____	_____	_____
_____	_____	_____
_____	_____	_____
_____	_____	_____

THE HEART OF INNOVATION

Not all conflict is bad. In fact, differences of opinion can be at the heart of some great outputs and innovations. Think about it. If you have a group of like-minded individuals with no disagreements, you are not likely to challenge the conventional. Although the process to reach finality might have been a smoother one, the output may be inferior.

Several years ago, I was brought into a financial services organization to review a virtual team that had just delivered one of the best returns on investment for a financial product that the company had ever seen. For them, "virtual" did not simply mean that the team was geographically dispersed; it also represented the fluidity of team members. The team comprised leaders and subject-matter experts from across various internal departments. There was unlimited potential for territoriality, disagreement, and conflict. But none of that became a distraction for the team. Senior leaders wanted to know what had contributed to the effectiveness so that they could replicate it. As it turned out, one of the most important aspects contributing to the team's success was the differences among the members.

Think about how you *have* utilized or *could* utilize individual differences constructively. What are some specific situations that have benefited or could benefit from multiple perspectives? What can you do to foster the encouragement of multiple perspectives? What are the challenges of facilitating multiple perspectives? How could you be prepared and overcome some of these challenges?

Situation (described and your role)	Potential Benefit (+) and Barrier (−)	Action
_____	_____	_____
_____	_____	_____
_____	_____	_____
_____	_____	_____
_____	_____	_____

Bob Contemplates Conflict

Bob seems to have avoided much conflict, including the good stuff that comes from such differences as experienced by the financial services team described above. His lone ranger posture was strong enough to discourage disagreement, and he never moved from simple staff management into a real strategic team leadership role.

"Bob, describe conflict to me. Is it something to be avoided at all cost?" I asked him.

"Well, conflict is a distraction, Tim. I think I avoid it. I just want to get things done. I know how to apply what I know to 'no drama' management."

"So let me ask you this," I said. "Did you ever invite the other project leaders to have sort of a generic meeting, a learning or sharing session, about typical project management problems, you know, whatever the usual stuff is, just to see how they handled such things—such as conflicting information, or conflicting approaches, or conflict with management above? Did you ever notice the others, like the people at your lunch, going off to a meeting room?"

"No, I can't think of a time ... no, I don't recall that," he answered sheepishly.

"It might be that no one wants to tangle with your expertise, or your view of your expertise. But maybe someone noticed their interest in generic problem solving, and one or two got a big promotion. Continue bouncing around companies or learn how to deal with conflict, Bob. It's there, outside of us and sometimes inside of us. In life, three things are certain: death, taxes ... and conflict. We all need to deal with it, including our conflicting views of ourselves."

Quick Tips

Quick Tips

To Prepare for Conflict

1. Conflict is inevitable. Perhaps more than results, how you react or respond to conflict or adversity will define you as a leader.

2. Find a mechanism or process by which you can deal with conflict constructively.

3. Be proactive in responding to conflict. It may not come naturally or comfortably, but if you can handle conflict well, it will greatly help your leadership story and build positive relationships.

STEP 4

Develop Your Theme

The theme of a leadership story is about characteristics and competence. It is what you do well and perhaps not so well, and, once again, self-awareness of it is essential. Self-awareness and acceptance of boundaries is the pathway to freedom. Knowing your abilities and even your limitations—regarding what you are capable of, interested in, and willing to do—can be quite liberating.

Let's compare the theme of your leadership story to books, movies, or even branded products. George Orwell's classic *1984* was about total control and how Big Brother used language to deceive people about his control.[11] That's how we remember the book and the two movies made from it. The theme of the movie *Jaws* is about how a community worked together, ordinary people and a couple of characters, to defeat the source of a summer disaster. When the key characters were on a fishing boat searching for the shark and saw it for the first time, they realized that their boat was not going to be sufficient to catch it. They did not have the needed capabilities or resources to accomplish their mission. That's how we think of it and how we, too, might someday need a bigger boat. When we think of CNN, we think of constant news coverage around the world. When we think of Google, we think of a search tool that seems to understand how we think and want to search. So, if you left your current company, how would those folks think of you? What would be their top-of-mind recollection of you? That's the theme of your leadership story.

The acceptance of our limitations opens the path to leadership. In his book *Long Walk to Freedom,* Nelson Mandela notes that it is what we make out of what we are, not what we are given, that separates one person from another.[12] So, if we are all different, our themes vary. As a leader, you need to be particularly careful to avoid being something you are not. Your theme is a great source of credibility in your leadership story.

I cannot think of a leader who knows more than everybody else in all aspects of the business. That's not to say there aren't leaders who *think* they know more than everybody. Some of the best leaders I've worked with ask questions more than they give direction and do not assume that they have all the answers. And here is the important part: they *listen.* They have opinions and can make decisions, to be sure, but they engage others in the process.

However, theme is more than what you know. When it comes to your leadership story, theme comprises your personality characteristics, attitude, technical skills, and interpersonal skills. There are a variety of leadership competency models. I am not advocating one over the other, as many have their merits. I encourage you to be aware of your leadership skills, as well as other key technical skills. However, there is a fine balance because leadership is about moving beyond the technical skills. You must let go of your expertise and comfort zone in order to truly embrace leadership.

Your role as a leader is to be aware of the skills, characteristics, and attributes that are important for leadership in your organization, and to know how you are doing relative to them. Is leadership only about *what* is accomplished, or does *how* the work is accomplished matter? The first is about churning out tasks, projects, and initiatives. I am not suggesting that the work is not important. However, when it comes to being a leader, the work itself is only part of the equation. How the work is accomplished is also important. And, perhaps most important, what are the skills and characteristics required for both? To be an effective leader and craft a complete story, you need both. As leaders, we are generally held accountable for accomplishing tasks—high quality, on time, on budget, and so on—and you always need to keep people in mind.

As a good leader, you need to recognize that different people require different approaches to leadership that may require you to have a different level of emotional intelligence and an adaptable skill set. For example, most leaders are inclined to lead as they would want to be led. Some team members may prefer direction and guidance to autonomy. Without this awareness, your actions may be interpreted quite differently than you intended.

For example, one leader I worked with, Bill, was a strong advocate of delegating down as far as possible. This was the manifestation of his value of trusting the experts on his team. It almost backfired in his leadership story. Bill regularly reviewed and tracked his company's financial statements, as he thought he should. But he also had staff members who were dedicated to the financial operations of the business. At a meeting where Bill was not involved, a leader outside of Bill's department asked if he was aware of the current financial reports. His team member who was responsible for financial operations responded, "Bill does not get involved in the details."

Well, that quickly became part of Bill's leadership story whether he liked it or not. And even though he had heard that not being involved in the details had become part of his story and was actively trying to correct that perception, it took him almost a year to change that aspect of his story. In life, stuff lingers. One of the lessons Bill took away from the experience was to fully understand what the organization believed was important, not just what he valued as a leader.

His story was being written based on the needs of others rather than on his beliefs or actions. Left as it was, this could have derailed Bill and undermined his intended leadership story or even the story he thought he was projecting. He was fortunate that he received feedback about this new element of his leadership story.

The other critical aspect of theme relative to your leadership story is feedback. You must seek feedback about how well you are doing. The story above illustrates just how easy it is to think you are doing well in an area when someone, somewhere else in the organization, does not. You might be showing up (a) differently than you think you are and (b) differently among different groups. So it is not enough to have the skills to be a leader; once again, your story is subject to the interpretations of others. Personally, I would rather know this than not know it, so that I can take action to be aware, as a leader, of how my theme is showing up.

Although there are many ways to get feedback on your leadership skills, characteristics, and traits, I have found that the best approach to feedback for leaders is a 360 assessment. It should be conducted anonymously for the most honest feedback. This is a useful leadership development tool that can allow you greater insights into how a variety of others (direct reports, boss, peers, and customers) think you are doing as a leader. It is useful to map your perceptions against theirs to determine where there might be dissonance and where you might prioritize development of your leadership skills.

I was having a conversation with one leader, Barry, who was a director in his company. If you had asked him how he was doing on the leadership and technical fronts, he would have given himself straight A's. He thought he was doing exceptionally well in all categories. He thought he was an excellent leader known for results and providing people with little direction and much autonomy. He thought he was a hands-off leader known for taking initiative and getting the job done.

But Barry received feedback indicating that he was perceived by others as a renegade type who was overconfident and often rolled over people in meetings. Some of his direct reports felt that he was not interested in them.

Barry went into panic mode. He did not want to be perceived that way at all. He knew this was not going to be turned around overnight. It would require time and conscious effort. First, he accepted the feedback. Second, he came up with a plan, which began with letting his team members know that he recognized this perception and was going to change. He asked for their help and specifically encouraged them to tell him if he was going into the negative land. He made it a point to see everyone from his team every day—not to check up on them but to check in with them, to ask how each was doing. As he got to know them, he learned more about their goals and what he could do to support them. He was able to assign people to projects that matched their interests, capabilities, and goals.

It took almost nine months and many new habits, but Bill knew he was viewed differently when he got feedback that there were two people who wanted to transfer onto his team because they heard he was a good developer of others.

For many leaders, the results of a 360 assessment provide many insights into their leadership story. The results help to minimize blind spots. If possible, as a best practice, try to complete a 360 approximately every 18 months. Eighteen months can be a long time to wait for feedback, so in the activities section, you will find approaches to get feedback on a much more immediate and routine basis.

REFLECTIVE QUESTIONS TO THINK ABOUT PLOT

1. What are you known for as a leader (skills, behaviors, attitudes)?
2. What do you want to be known for?
3. What are your strengths and areas for development as a leader?
4. What traits, behaviors, and characteristics are you most proud of as a leader?
5. How do you continuously develop yourself as a leader and teach others?

Activities to Develop Your Theme

Activity	For Self	Give to Others
Give Yourself a Grade	✓	✓
Greatest Hits (and Misses)	✓	
Keep a Diary	✓	
Moving On	✓	
The Mirror	✓	✓

GIVE YOURSELF A GRADE

Feedback can be difficult to come by. For a leader, honest, candid feedback can be even more difficult to come by. But feedback is critical for course correction and continuous development. As a quick way to get feedback, I encourage leaders to give themselves a grade, just as if they were in school, *A* through *F.* Of course, the assumption is that you will be honest with yourself. And we know that self-report data has its limitations. But it is a step in the right direction if done honestly.

This kind of feedback can be done on a variety of topics. For example, you can give yourself a grade for how you delivered a presentation, how you gave feedback to an employee, how you interacted with your boss, or any number of occurrences throughout the day. You can give yourself a grade for the day for how well you did overall as a leader.

The key to this is to include in your thought process why you are giving yourself a particular grade. What did you do to deserve that *A* or *C* or whichever grade you earned? And your criteria should span not just what you think but also how you think others reacted to it and how it was viewed within the context of the organization. To close out the activity, ask yourself what you would do the same or differently in the future.

There are two variations on this exercise. The first is that you ask someone else to give you a grade and explain why you earned that grade. It is often difficult to put people on the spot for some potentially difficult conversations. But if you are open about giving yourself a grade first and are reasonably critical, you might create a level of comfort and willingness for others to provide you input. Start by saying what grade you gave yourself and why. The real benefit here is that you are showing some humility and vulnerability as a leader and an openness to receiving feedback.

The second variation, a much more conservative approach, is to give others a grade. I recommend doing this internally—meaning in your own mind—and being thoughtful about the criteria you used to give the grade. Why did you give them a particular grade? What would you have done differently? What can you learn from them? Using this activity, you can learn a great deal from others.

GREATEST HITS (AND MISSES)

Your leadership story to this point has likely been filled with ups and downs, hits and misses, successes and failures. You have the opportunity to learn from both the positive and negative experiences. For this activity, write down your greatest two or three hits. These are professional or personal accomplishments that say something about you as a person. Describe the accomplishments. What made them great? And what did you learn?

Do the same for your greatest misses. What was your greatest disappointment? What made it so? What was your role in these experiences? Be as specific as possible, and think about the turning points for each, what your role was, and what you would do the same and differently in the future.

Greatest Hits

Hit	What Made It Great Was	What I Learned Was
_____	_____	_____
_____	_____	_____
_____	_____	_____

Greatest Misses

Hit	What Made It a Miss Was	What I Learned Was
_____	_____	_____
_____	_____	_____
_____	_____	_____

What two or three things would you do the same if faced with a similar opportunity? Why?

_____

_____

What two or three things would you do differently if faced with a similar opportunity? Why?

_____

_____

KEEP A DIARY

As a leader, you are likely involved in a number of projects throughout the year. Some leaders may be involved in so many projects that they cannot remember them all. In some cases, you may be defined, and your leadership story may be written, by your success and failures.

For this activity, you should keep a running list of the projects you worked on throughout the year. Although you can adapt the headings that you track, think about including the project name, a one- or two-sentence description, your role, the dates, and anything else notable, such as outcomes, awards, or recognition. Think about this in terms of what you did, what you learned, and what you taught.

Project (name, description, dates)	Team Members (my role)	Outcomes
_____	_____	_____
_____	_____	_____
_____	_____	_____

This will greatly help you to recall the work you have been part of, accomplishments, and any lessons learned. It is important because if you can't recall what you have worked on and where you have added value to the business, you can't expect others to remember either. This also becomes a useful tool for your annual performance evaluation.

Additionally, it provides a good check and balance for your involvement as a leader. If you find that your list is running low, look for ways to get more involved. If there is too much on your list, look for ways to engage others in some projects. It will give them exposure and experience, and you will be viewed as a developer of others.

MOVING ON

Your career is a journey during which you will impact and be impacted by many people. You will also learn a lot along the way, and hopefully you view the imparting of knowledge as part of your role as leader. Whether you are changing jobs within the same organization, moving to a new organization, or retiring, what do you want your legacy to be as you transition from one place to the next? What do you want to be known for? Let's hope that theme is positive.

This activity is about awareness and planning. For this activity, imagine that you are transitioning out of your current role. You have asked a colleague who knows you well to give a short speech at your farewell reception.

- What do you want him or her to say about you?
- What do you want to be known for as a leader?
- Where is it most important that you be successful as a leader? As a person?
- What aspects of your leadership story will you be most proud of if they come to fruition?
- Where would you have the greatest regrets if that part of your leadership story were left unfulfilled?

To make this activity real, consider writing out your farewell speech in fewer than 500 words. Does your speech change if it is for your retirement? Does your speech change if it is at the end of your life? Your legacy spans more than work, and I encourage you to think about the broader legacy you wish to leave. What are you doing to contribute to your legacy? What specific actions do you need to take to build the legacy you wish to have? In the space below, be specific, and be concise.

I want to be known for . . .   I need to . . .

_____   _____
_____   _____
_____   _____
_____   _____
_____   _____
_____   _____

THE MIRROR

When you look in the mirror, what do you see? What if the mirror displays only skills and abilities rather than physical attributes? Now what do you see? What do others see when they look at you?

This activity is adapted from Arneson's *Bootstrap Leadership.* He states that people carry around your brand in a few words. In the first column below, in five to seven words, write the words you would use to describe yourself as a leader. In the second column, write down five to seven words for how you think others would describe your leadership style. And in the third column, write down five to seven words to describe your ideal leadership style.

I see myself as . . .	Others see me as . . .	I would like to be known as . . .
_____	_____	_____
_____	_____	_____
_____	_____	_____
_____	_____	_____
_____	_____	_____
_____	_____	_____
_____	_____	_____

Now, without sharing your list, ask several others from a variety of groups to describe you as a leader in five to seven adjectives.

How would you describe me as a leader?

_____

When you look across all three of your columns, what stands out? Are there more similarities or differences across the columns? What is the difference between your perceptions and others'? Why is there a difference? What are the differences between your current leadership and your ideal leadership? Why? What are you prepared to do about it?

In order to become the ideal leader I want to be, I will...

_____

_____

In order to better align who I am as a leader with how others see me, I will...

_____

_____

Bob Thinks about Theme

If you are still uncertain about how to pull this together, Bob is in the same boat. But at his farewell lunch, he did get an idea of what leadership story theme he was leaving behind as he jumped ship to another company.

"Bob, I'm going to give you a choice between two doors ... and, no, no tigers behind one of them," I assured him. "You can continue being a good technocrat who rules his project domain with one or two direct reports. Given that you are in your 40s, you could play the same tech-guru role at four or five more companies before you hang up your certification. Or, you could hire and mold bigger teams with strategic assignments that are closely watched at the CEO level, help develop others to their potential, and maybe even get some big stock or option awards. And not have to go to a new company. Instead, learn new things in product lines the company never dreamed of. What's your choice?"

Bob sat there for a while. "I see your point, Tim. I am uncomfortable with moving around a lot, but it's because I am too comfortable being the project expert, holding on to it. I've been wearing my expertise hat all my career. People know me for that right now. So maybe I am identifying an issue for myself: when do I wear my expert hat, and when do I wear a leader hat?"

"And that's how people think of you, Bob. They said so, however uncomfortably, at your farewell luncheon. Do you want that lone ranger stuff to be the theme of your leadership story? If you do, it's going to follow you, not just sit with former colleagues. Maybe follow you for years. People talk, and social media gives negative talk an infinite lifespan."

Bob was listening carefully.

Quick Tips

To Develop Your Theme

1. For quick feedback, give yourself and others a grade; ask others to do the same. It can help initiate candid conversations, reinforce expectations, and highlight perceptions.

2. Effective leadership requires you to let go of (or delegate) some technical skills and embrace your role as leader.

3. Reconcile how you think you are doing as a leader with how others perceive you are doing.

STEP 5

Find Your Optimal Setting

When it comes to story, setting refers to where the events of the story take place. The setting for your leadership story is about geographical location and the organization you work for, and it is also about the work itself. Specifically, for part of your leadership story, you will need to determine how the setting of your work provides meaning to you. You should consider how the setting contributes positively or negatively to your leadership story.

No right or wrong answer exists for the question of whether you are in the right setting, except for one qualifier: How's it working for you? If you answer something along the lines of "Not so good," then it is up to you to think about why that is so and what you are prepared to do about it.

I worked with an established leader who had made a career change a year prior. She was a midcareer leader who had taken a job at a flower shop because she wanted to be around something beautiful and help bring joy to people every day. Although I did not know her before she worked at the flower shop, she explained how she had never been happier. She also reminded me that it was a tough decision, and the decision required some sacrifices. That is an extreme example, and I am not encouraging you to quit your job. What I am encouraging you to do is *find your flower shop*—that environment that brings out the best in you and others. Look for opportunities to create it within your existing environment.

For many of us, our story has evolved in a variety of settings over time and may continue to evolve. Even if we don't change settings, the environment around us might change, so we still must be aware of our setting and how it is working for us. You should also consider how you as a leader foster a sense of pride in the work you do and where you do it (i.e., organization, physical setting).

Think about when you arrive in an organization for the first time. You are likely confronted with stories about people currently and formerly part of the organization. You understand what gets rewarded and what gets punished. That forms the basis of the organization's culture, and it also serves as data for you to better understand what is important within this new setting. If you have been part of an organization for some time, you have likely contributed to the stories in some way. How have you been and can you be a protagonist for your setting and in your setting?

Setting needs to be monitored for the effect that you have on it and it has on you. The setting should not be a source of or grounds for conflict. As a leader, you need to know what is important to you, what is enabling, and what is constraining. You need to have a long-term plan regarding where you want to be and an understanding of where you are at your best. Having a good understanding of the elements of your leadership story up until this point will provide a great deal of clarity when it comes to the reflective questions included throughout this chapter.

Sometimes your leadership story is not reflecting you accurately or where you want it to be, either personally or in the eyes of others. I'm not advocating changing settings, although that may be necessary at some point. Keep in mind the saying "The grass is always greener on the other side of the hill." The truth of the matter is that the grass is greener where you water it. So what are you prepared to do to create an environment that allows you and others to be your best?

However, this is more about utilizing opportunities when they exist. Specifically, when you are on a new team or in a new organization, you have the opportunity to revise your leadership story. You need to be prepared to take advantage of those opportunities, and it begins with having a complete picture of your leadership story—where it is currently and where you want it to be. So it may be best in many circumstances to make the most of what you have. In fact, my first recommendation would be for you to make the most of your current situation. It may require some difficult conversations relative to your needs and expectations.

In any event, I am advocating that you take a close look at your setting—that you examine what has had an effect on you, what contributes to or inhibits you from being at your best, and where you might see yourself in the long term. What is important to you? Where can you be at your best? And how can you take the necessary steps to achieve your goals? What can you do to make your setting better?

Dawn had been in her organization for more than seven years and in her current role for almost five years. She had her routine down, from her drive into work to her office setup to her daily and weekly routines interacting with her team. People tended to come in and work with their heads down and then go home. Little day-to-day inspiration existed, and the office space was a generic, somber, sober gray. It had always been that way. She never questioned it, and neither did anyone from her team.

She recently hired Sara for a creative role that was open on her team. Sara had a ton of energy, but the bland office environment didn't nurture a creative spirit. She was ready to work hard but needed stimulus and exchange. One day, Sara asked Dawn if it was OK to bring in personal pictures to put in her work space. Sara loved to travel. She brought in pictures from a whitewater-rafting trip, a rock-climbing adventure, and her family beach vacation. Sara loved anything to do with water and especially loved lighthouses, so she brought in mini-statues of three of her favorite ones. Other colleagues noticed the difference and brought in family and pet pictures, pictures of their trips, and other items of personal interest. A few brought in small plants. One even decorated her workspace for the various seasons.

Something interesting happened. People began to walk around the office, share personal stories and interests, and exchange ideas about all kinds of things, personal and business. Because of Sara's yearning for a more energetic environment, a more positive and productive attitude radiated throughout the office.

Are you where you want to be—geographically, emotionally, and organizationally? Where you are geographically and culturally at this stage in your career will influence the questions you ask and the answers you give. For example, if balance is important, how does your setting contribute to that? In another example, if you are in the early stages of your career, you may have a greater sense of adventure and flexibility. At another stage in your career, it might be more important for you to have stability. Neither is wrong; they are just different.

When you look back at where you have been, which settings have had a great impact on you? Why? Was it the people or the place? Was it the structures, policies, or culture? What have you learned? And how do you realize the impacts of where you have been and where you are—all aspects of your setting—on your leadership story?

When you look ahead, where do you want to be, in terms of location, life, and career stage? Be thoughtful about what will allow you to be at your best and achieve your goals. True, you might have to make some trade-offs along the way. But it is better for you to drive that process according to your needs and goals.

REFLECTIVE QUESTIONS TO THINK ABOUT YOUR OPTIMAL SETTING

1. How does your setting enable or constrain your best leadership capabilities?
2. What gets rewarded and punished in your organization?
3. How have your travels shaped your perspective as a leader? Where have you been that has influenced your thinking?
4. How can you make the most of your current setting?
5. Where have you had the greatest impact and experienced the greatest satisfaction as a leader? Why?

Activities to Find Your Optimal Setting

Activity	For Self	Give to Others
Masterful 2x2	✓	
Detour!	✓	
New Construction	✓	✓
Gratitude	✓	
Be Self-a-Where and S.M.A.R.T.	✓	✓

MASTERFUL 2x2

Most jobs have aspects that we like and some that we don't. They also have things we are good at and things we are not. In those same instances, there are several aspects that are critical to your role. For example, you may love being an accountant, and you might be good at it. But if it is not critical to your leadership role, you may find yourself micromanaging and not delegating where you should, which, I assure you, will reflect on your leadership story.

Because this concerns your leadership story, it is important that you have self-awareness about it. The result of being self-aware will help you to focus your efforts. This activity is about identifying and becoming a master of what you love to do.

First, in the 2x2 matrix that follows, write down the aspects of your job that fit in each quadrant. Keep in mind that some of the work may be important to the organization or your role, so it is less likely that you would simply stop doing some aspects of your job. On the other hand, you need to be aware of what you like and what you are good at (and the variations) in order to best position your leadership story. For example, if you spend your time in the upper right quadrant, you are likely to be excited and deliver great results, and you will see benefits through your leadership story. If you spend time in the bottom left quadrant, you are more likely to be disengaged and make mistakes that will reflect negatively on your leadership story.

	Like/Important for Role	
Good/Important for Role Yes	Teach others	Become a master of your craft
No	Stop/delegate	Learn/develop
	No	Yes

When you are done, write down a plan to harness the positive aspects you have listed and mitigate any of the negative aspects. Think in terms of becoming a master and being a developer of others.

Harness the positive. I've talked about the importance of technical expertise throughout this book. You've got to be technically competent and know the business in order to be recognized as someone with future leadership potential. Your technical capability is very likely one of the reasons you are given greater leadership responsibilities. So it can be hard to shift from the "doing" mindset of a technical expert to the "developing" mind-set of a leader.

As you become a leader and ultimately take on greater leadership responsibilities, you will be faced with new challenges and decisions about what you need to focus on. Just as you worked hard to become a great technical expert, to become a great leader you must shift some of your focus, planning, and effort to leadership. Time spent on some of the procedural details should shift to a greater focus on setting a vision, charting the course, listening, deciding, motivating, and developing. To do this, you must let go of some of your technical responsibilities. You must delegate. You must also teach and develop others. How will you continue to develop and pass along what you are good at and like to do? How and what will you teach others? And how and what should you learn and develop? Be specific.

Mitigate the negative. How can you delegate work that you don't like and are not good at? Note: this may be a development opportunity for others on your team.

DETOUR!

I live in the city, and it seems that roadwork is always going on somewhere. The city claims that it is in the name of progress, to make things better. But I typically find it an inconvenience unless I know about it beforehand and find an alternate route. One thing I have learned about these detours is the absence of shortcuts. You simply have to plan for them and work around them. Somehow, I always end up at my destination.

When it comes to your leadership story, your setting is no different. I know of few people who have everything perfect around their setting. Something can always be done to make the setting better.

For this activity, start by listing anything you would consider a roadblock in your setting. Rate it on a scale of 1 to 5 (5 is for the biggest impediment to your being at your best as a leader). And then briefly note any mitigating strategies. In other words, list what you might be able to do either to change that aspect of the setting or detour around it. Note, this is not about people; it should focus on the physical setting, culture, policies, structures, and the like.

Roadblock	Rating	Strategies for Change or Detour
_____	_____	_____
_____	_____	_____
_____	_____	_____
_____	_____	_____

NEW CONSTRUCTION

This is an extension of the Detour! activity above. However, this focuses on those aspects of setting within your control that you can adapt to allow you to be your best.

Without consideration of your current setting, think about what you need to be at your best. Do you need music? Do art or personal photographs energize you and make you happy? Do you need to stand up and move around throughout the day? Do you need fresh air? What kind of setting, including time of day, do you find most conducive to creative problem solving, especially about people issues? Focus on the things over which you might have some control.

For example, if the beach makes you happy, that is nice (it makes me happy, too) but not relevant to adapting your setting to better meet your needs. This activity is not just about what makes you happy. This is about what needs to be present for you to be at your best and what you might be able to do about it. Keep in mind, it may require a conversation with a supervisor. It may take time or be incremental. To manage expectations, also keep in mind the importance of fairness and equity within the workplace.

I am at my best when . . .	To move in that direction, I will . . .
_____	_____
_____	_____
_____	_____
_____	_____
_____	_____

To extend this activity, you should also ask others to describe when you are at your best and the impact it has. What are the situations? How does it show? And how does that impact others?

Examples of When I Am at My Best	And the Impact That It Has
_____	_____
_____	_____
_____	_____
_____	_____
_____	_____

GRATITUDE

Sometimes we don't realize how fortunate we are. The good in our lives becomes wallpaper—background that we take for granted and hardly notice. I have found in my experience that we are literally surrounded by good. We just have to look for it, recognize it, and pay attention to it.

Yes. It's back again. For this gratitude activity, your focus is on your setting rather than on people. Every day for a week, for one minute, write down all the things you are grateful for in your setting. You can refer to past or present aspects, but they have to be real, *and they have to be about your setting.* The simple question is: what are you thankful for in your setting? For this activity, you should think about the physical environment you work in, aspects of the corporate and local culture you are part of, perhaps your local geography, and the like.

BE SELF-A-WHERE AND S.M.A.R.T.

To be at your best, where do you need to be, and what do you need to do? We all have an environment that allows us to be at our best, to do our best thinking, to reflect, or to be creative. There may be different places for each of those activities. In fact, it may be a place, a time, or a set of conditions (for example, listening to music might help you to be creative). These are all noble pursuits, and they may be critical to the future of your leadership story. But we often don't make time for what we view as important.

For this activity, first list what you wish you did more of. These could include reflection, fitness, creativity, planning, or any number of things you would like to incorporate into your routine or spend more time on. Then, rate the importance of these activities for you to be at your best (1 to 5, with 1 being most important). Next, write down the amount of time you would need to spend on each activity. Finally, write down a realistic and measurable plan to find more time for what you need to do or where you need to be to make it happen. Not just what you will commit to, but how you will make it happen.

There really is no wrong answer. This is about creating self-awareness around what you need to be at your best. It is about what is most important to you and about identifying specific, measurable, actionable, realistic, and tangible (S.M.A.R.T.) goals to get you there.

Activity	Rating	Time	S.M.A.R.T. Goal

As a leader, you need to create an environment that allows others to be at their best. For the next part of this activity, identify specific individuals and what they need in order to be at their best, how you currently enable or constrain them, and what you can do to support them. Ask each member of your team to answer the two questions below, and have a conversation with each of them about their responses. You may want to provide some context around what you or the employee can control. For example, I once worked with a leader who tried this activity without any guidelines, and many of the responses centered around having greater access to parking near the office. That is interesting for discussion, but the leader was unable to take specific action. Note that this is about being a supportive leader, not about establishing codependence. It should lead to a dialogue about and awareness of individual priorities and your role as leader.

What do you need in order to be at your best?

_____

_____

How do I enable or constrain you from being at your best?

_____

_____

Bob Explores His Setting

I talked with Bob about the role that setting plays in people's work environments and the often-negative effects of settings. We discussed how Michael Bloomberg completely changed the floor plan in the executive wing of New York's City Hall when he became mayor. He insisted on being in a cubicle among the staff, in the center of the large room. Communication was important to him. After all, he had set up a communications empire. It wasn't about cost, it was about access—the staff's access to him and his access to them.

"Well, we pretty much all have cubes, some bigger than others," Bob observed.

"OK, but setting is several things, just like in a story," I said. "It's physical; it's time of year and time of day. In a leadership story, the setting can enhance your ability to lead and affect the comfort level of those you try to lead. It's about the ease of being able to say to someone, 'Hey, let's go get a cup of coffee and talk about that issue.'"

"My direct reports can come talk. We use Outlook to schedule appointments. I'm available," he assured me.

"Let me change gears here, Bob. Imagine a small business—say, 10 people. The owner is an autocrat. He frequently reminds everyone that it's his ballgame. When people speak up or offer a suggestion—or, worse, a contrary viewpoint—they all get the ballgame speech. He's a leader, all right. He's definitely displaying the airs of one of the leadership types I've talked about.

But how comfortable is that environment? How many sick days do you think people take? How many are there after 5p.m.? Get my point?"

"Tim, I am not that way, not at all..."

"I didn't say you were. Let's make that owner a 1 on a 1-to-10 scale of leadership. He ain't leading! Let's say that Mayor Bloomberg, in business and in politics, was a 10, just for the sake of discussion, OK? Bob, where are you on that continuum regarding the setting, the comfort level, the warm and fuzzies, of your leadership? And another thing: Outlook is great, a very productive tool. But it's just a tool! Using it that way for appointments is just telling people that they have to approach you—dare I say crawl to you?—and, with luck, find an open slot on your Outlook calendar to talk with you. That's one-directional. When was the last time you just popped in on someone and said, 'How's it going with your project?'"

Bob had never quite thought of his little corner of the company cube farm in those terms.

Quick Tips

To Find Your Optimal Setting

1. Take ownership and responsibility for what you can do to make your setting optimal for you.

2. Know and articulate what about a setting enables you to be at your best and constrains you from the same.

3. Actively seek feedback from your team members about what it takes for them to be at their best, and have a specific plan to help support them.

CHAPTER III

The Narrative Arc

Let's pause for a moment here. We've discussed the elements common to any story, and your leadership story can't be an interesting one unless it covers those basic elements. What's more, it won't be much of a story unless it has a beginning, middle, and end—a timeline. This is called a *narrative arc,* with rising action that reaches a big turning point, or climax, and descending action. Movies follow the same pattern, or we wouldn't be eager to see that next film.

Your arc should lead to a high point in your career when everything comes together. Now is the time to think about where you want to go with your leadership—or your purpose—and how you are going to get there—or your path. Your arc weaves its way through all the other elements of your story. As you look across each of the elements, think about it in terms of your timeline and the influence that certain people and events have had on the way you think and act as a leader.

Mapping Your Arc and Discovering Your Leadership Truths

Confucius said, "Study the past if you wish to define the future." The past is a foundational aspect of our leadership story, and it shows up today as our leadership mind-set. It is important to understand the past and how it shapes our leadership story—to reflect on it, to learn from it, but not to live in it. Who or what has shaped your most deeply held values as a leader?

When it comes to how this manifests itself in our leadership, there are the stories we tell ourselves—from our inner voice or mind-set—to justify and rationalize our actions. And then there are the outward-facing stories that others hear and by which they judge our leadership. How well do your inner and outer voices align? Put more bluntly, is what you tell yourself a stretch from what others perceive? Would you agree that it is important to assess the match? Remember how shocked Bob was at lunch?

So where are you on your leadership journey? This is an opportunity to look in the mirror. As we transition from understanding your story to communicating it, this section gives you a chance to map out your leadership timeline in order to visualize your narrative arc. Sure, this sounds easy enough, but it can be a little uncomfortable. You certainly could skim the surface and have a superficial arc. If you really want to have a deeper understanding of your leadership, you will have to work hard on this activity.

Think about your significant personal milestones—those events and people that had a significant impact on what you value and how you think as a leader. This will allow you to measure your milestones and guideposts along the way to your ultimate goal. It is an opportunity to look back and make sense of the people, places, and events that have contributed to your leadership story in general, and your mind-set or voice in particular.

Here is how this works. There is really no rule as to timeline format. You may chart a line across the page, write a narrative, or put your story in outline form in bullet points. I prefer to start with an outline, and I like to work chronologically up to the present.

I have found it best to segment one's life—particularly for the early years. In part one of this activity, think about your first 15 to 20 years. Who were the instrumental people in your life? I suggest beginning close to your inner circle and moving outward. Were there parents, grandparents, siblings, or other family members who had a strong influence on you? As you work your way out from family, were others influential, such as camp counselors, coaches, church or community leaders, or teachers? Make a note of who they were and how they influenced you. Most important, what was it about their leadership that you remember? Keep in mind that you are not looking for volume. You are looking for influence.

Person/Event	How It Impacted Me/ What I Learned
Name of person or short description of the event	Summary of what you learned —about people, responsibility, leadership, and yourself

In part two of this activity, adding to the record you've been creating above, think about the events and activities since your early years that have influenced your deepest thinking as a leader—that had a lasting impact on you. They could be single events or something that occurred over time. Think about times when you took on responsibility for people and when others looked to you for guidance and direction. How did you act? What did that teach you about people? About being a leader? What did you learn about yourself and other people?

As you continue with the activity up to the present day, you may find it easiest to continue across time segments (e.g., every 10 years), or you may be more comfortable shifting your focus to the key people and events that have influenced how you think about leadership. Either approach is fine, and I would encourage you to keep two things in mind as you document. First, this activity always encourages impact over quantity. Second, your story is best represented in chronological order. Why? You may rediscover that your leadership is anchored in some core principles grounded at a very young age.

You may like what you find ... or you may not. The task is not to rationalize or explain away what you find about your core principles; it is to understand your leadership truths. This activity is not meant to indicate anything right or wrong, per se. It is about gaining a deeper understanding of what has shaped you as a leader.

As you complete the timeline activity, you should begin to have greater clarity about your leadership truths than ever before. Do you like where you are in your leadership journey? Do you like your story? As you look to the future, what path is your arc taking? Is there still much work to be done? The extent to which there is dissonance between who you are today and who you want to be as a leader provides the starting point for your personal development.

While much of this section is focused on what has shaped your deepest thinking and values as a leader, you should take the time to think about the role you play in other people's arcs. What impact are you having on others? Steve Jobs's leadership style is well documented. Although he got results that continue to be admired, he left a lot of personal casualties in his wake. Imagine the power of the ongoing impact he would have had if he had not only developed innovative products but also developed his people to a greater extent. When all is said and done, you will be remembered for the people you influenced and molded, but only incidentally for the tasks and projects you checked off. What do you want to be remembered for? How are you using your leadership for the greater good?

Here's another tip. It's the opposite of forecasting. It's called *backcasting.* Imagine where you want your leadership timeline to end up, in the future. Start with the ideal you really want. Now go backward in some increment—say, five years. What do you have to do to meet that benchmark before you can reach the end goal? Maybe the increments are shorter, such as a year. Whatever works for you. Then keep going—e.g., by another year or five-year space. Keep backcasting until you reach, well, today, marking off each sub-accomplishment that you know you need before the end of the timeline. Does this give you more of a leadership plan than you had, say, one hour ago?

Bob's Narrative Arc

One evening, Bob and I took a long walk around the lake near the conference center where I was speaking. Walking is a great way to free up thinking.

"Bob, I often talk about a person's inner voice and outer voice. The way you were at the lunch with your peers at the last company was your outer voice. It clashed with your inner voice, the one you were talking to yourself with. Do you see what I am getting at?" I asked him.

"Well, Tim, I am quite aware of the lunch and its impact, OK?" he said, somewhat in frustration.

"Sure. Enough of the lunch, already. So let's go back in time and find some more inner voices and outer voices, way back when, and see how we can build a narrative arc for your leadership story," I suggested.

About then, we passed a bunch of geese on the lake. We stopped and stared. Not many geese here in Washington or Bob's home city. Suddenly, Bob made a comment that was robust with opportunity.

"Gee, isn't it funny how the whole bunch of them follow that one guy all over the lake? I've always wondered about that in birds."

I decided to hold that thought for a while. Then I explained to Bob how the narrative arc reaches a high point in a career and how what leads up to that arc is quite influential in our professional lives. We discussed the fact that the inner voice is the one we use to rationalize our own story to ourselves, but the outer voice is what others are saying. Conflict sometimes happens.

"Bob, who influenced you in your youth? Not who persuaded you to enter your current professional occupation, but, rather, who made an impact on how you thought about yourself?"

"Oh, I had a science teacher in high school who said something no one had ever said to me. It was a lab class and we were building small motorized catapults as examples of classic tools. I made a suggestion about something—can't remember what it was—and he told me I was a creative problem solver. He said I looked at the design we were all working from and questioned it. He thought my idea, as small as it was, demonstrated good thinking," Bob recalled. "He also said I was good at explaining difficult concepts simply. Funny, but I remember his saying that Einstein claimed anyone who couldn't explain something simply didn't understand it himself, and I have never forgotten that idea," he added.

"Anyone else? Think outside of school ... church, camp, parents, friends, sports, memorable conflicts ... what comes to mind?" I prodded.

"Well, a church leader, during a study session, said I asked good questions, although I don't think he appreciated some of them," Bob joked.

"Any crises or conflicts that became part of your inner voice?"

"Ah, yes. Summer camp one year. I was a student camp assistant or something. Turned out some kids had some conflict or maybe were from opposing gangs ... can't remember what. It was near getting physical, and we couldn't have that. The camp director was about to pounce, when, out of the blue, I offered the two groups a challenge: which group could build a Native American tepee that would withstand the storm we heard was coming? I don't know how I thought of it. I do recall the camp director staring at me and then smiling slightly," Bob recalled with a nostalgic grin.

"How did it work out? Did the storms, both of them, things down?" I pressed.

"Everything came out OK, and we had no problems. And both tepees withstood the rain, but each was built slightly differently, and we let each group describe how they made theirs," he recalled. "And whatever I proposed thereafter—for days—they all went along with it."

"They all went along with it?" I asked. "Why do you suppose that happened, Bob?"

"I guess I was turning good problem solving into an early stage of leadership," he observed.

We explored his timeline further, especially as he developed his professional, technical expertise. Bob liked being a problem solver in all his jobs. He found it fun. He liked asking questions to challenge conventional thinking. I wondered, why hadn't he developed his leadership skill too? For some reason, he defaulted, so to speak, to what his inner voice told him was the safe route. So I asked him about all that.

"Staying in my professional frame of mind was easy," Bob admitted. "Maybe it was the fear of the unknown about taking on big endeavors. Maybe I thought my luck would run out. After all, corporate life is not like a science lab or a summer-camp conflict. I guess I didn't want to fail at anything," he ventured.

"Bob, many management gurus have expressed a variation on this simple thought: if you never fail at some endeavor, you aren't taking enough risks—reasonable risks. All companies have failed products. So what if you call one wrong? You move on. Learn from it. GM failed with Saturn. MGM has produced hundreds of failed movies. Procter & Gamble regularly pulls the plug on consumer products. Failures provide pathways to successes. Edison spoke of this long ago. If you don't have a bomb now and then, someone upstairs will think you are playing too safe.

"It sounds like fear of failure is a key roadblock here. That, and a comfort level that is too comfortable. Don't get me wrong, Bob. Everyone wants to be comfortable, but it's also comforting—and fun—to lead other people into their creative potential. What's more, following a creative leader is fun. It's also comfortable. Those kids at camp almost got nasty, but then they followed you for days—because they wanted to, for whatever reason."

It was our third trip around the small lake. We again came across the geese. "They just seem comfortable following that lead gander, don't they?" Bob joked.

"Yup. Leadership is the art of making people feel comfortable with being led, giving them the sense that they are headed for what's good, something that's best," I said.

CHAPTER IV

The Art of Communicating Your Leadership Story

Understanding and aligning your leadership story is a foundational part of the equation. How you communicate your story tells as much about you as the story itself. If not told right, at the right opportunity and with the right audience, your leadership story can backfire.

Since your leadership story lives in your actions and the hearts, minds, and perceptions of others, it is important to think about, be aware of, and plan for how you communicate your leadership story. As the title of this section suggests, there is considerable art to communicating your story. There is no single best way.

If we agree that understanding your leadership story is complex and dynamic, telling it is equally so. In fact, adding to the complexity is that you may be telling your leadership story inadvertently. Or you may not even be the one telling your leadership story. Of course, you play a critical role in communicating your leadership story. And, your audience and your leadership story itself also play a critical role as well. To communicate your leadership story, you must think about and proactively plan for your messages (what), be aware of unique opportunities and timing (when, where, and how), and also recognize the role that others play in communicating your leadership story (who). You will also see that audience matters, and others can and should play a broader role in your leadership story.

Chapter 4 of this book provides a guide for you to think about your leadership story, as well as strategies to help you plan for communicating it. Each step in chapter 4 begins with an overview and explanation of a storytelling element. And because every situation, environment, and personal level of comfort with expressing your leadership story is different, each step provides questions to guide self-reflection and introduces strategies and tips to help you prepare to tell your leadership story. Because this deals with execution, you will find the strategies, techniques, and tips to be tactical in nature.

When you tell a story, several elements are required for it to have the greatest intended impact.

What Constitutes Good Storytelling?

To tell a good story, you must know your message, know the audience, make the most of opportunities to communicate your story, and recognize that actions speak louder than words; and you should enlist others to tell your story. For your intended message to come across and be memorable, you need to be true to yourself and authentic. Depending on your leadership story and your personal comfort level in communicating it, you may need to rely on some aspects of storytelling more than others.

Your leadership story is uniquely yours. And you need to be familiar with it. *Step 6* discusses the importance of knowing your message. Having just completed many of the activities earlier in the book, you should have greater self-awareness and greater insights into how others perceive you. This chapter provides guidance for pulling your story together in a succinct and crisp way.

Your leadership story needs to be flexible enough to meet the needs of a variety of audiences, whether large groups or individuals. *Step 7* discusses the potential audiences you should be prepared for at a minimum, the importance of understanding their needs, and how to tailor your message to your audience. You will be introduced to strategies and techniques to help you be ready to adjust your story to meet the needs of a variety of audiences.

Timing may not be everything, but it sure is important. There is a time and a place for everything. *Step 8* delves into why this is important and provides strategies for finding just the right opportunities—or moments of truth—to showcase your leadership story or an aspect of it. You will find that some opportunities can be planned, while others are unanticipated. Depending on the audience, these moments of truth may be highly unique events, so it is important that you be prepared for the unanticipated.

I wish that communicating your leadership story were as simple as verbally presenting who you are as a leader and what you believe in. Unfortunately, that is not the case. Much of your leadership story resides in your actions and other nonverbal cues. *Step 9* discusses this topic, providing examples and tips to increase your awareness, as well as strategies to actively engage your actions and other nonverbal communication to your advantage.

As we have discussed throughout this book, you are the owner of your leadership story. However, others play a critical role, whether in their perceptions or as a protagonist or antagonist. In *Step 10,* I discuss the broader role of others, as well as how and why to enlist them in telling your leadership story. The results can be quite powerful.

STEP 6

Know Your Message

Good storytellers have a purpose in mind. They know what they want to share and why. This may sound straightforward enough, but without specific strategies, it can be easier said than done.

Adding to the complexity, the message of your leadership story is not just about you. You may not even always be the main character. Great leaders engage others in their story. They ask questions and should strive to be known for the questions they ask. And they make strong connections. Your message must be simple, clear, understandable, and motivational. And, unlike folk tales, your leadership story should not exaggerate to make a point.

How you communicate your story is an important consideration as well. If you want your leadership story (or aspects of it) to be memorable, it needs to be succinct, timely, and inspiring. You have to think about your comfort zone in telling aspects of your leadership story, as well as where and how you can have the greatest impact with your message. In other words, you have to frame your message appropriately. For example, let's say an important element of your leadership story and a defining characteristic and value is that you are humble. You cannot very well go around telling people that you are humble. So throughout this chapter, you are provided with strategies to think about not only what you want to convey but how best to convey it.

Let's begin by focusing on what you want to convey. The first part of the book provided a number of activities to help you define important elements of your leadership story. You should have a solid point of view about who you are as a leader, what you value, and what has shaped your leadership story. Keep in mind that there may be elements of your leadership story that you want to convey and some aspects that you may not want to convey. Now that you have a broader understanding, think about the following questions to help you begin to home in on what you want to tell:

- How would you succinctly summarize your leadership story? Think about what you are most passionate about as a leader.
- What are the key aspects you want to reinforce? Think about this in terms of how you lead and interact with people, as well as the tasks.
- What lessons do you want to impart? Think about what messages you want to impart about yourself, your approach to leadership, what you have learned, and your expectations of yourself and others.
- Who can best help you communicate your leadership story? What messages do they need to know to do so effectively?

Framing Your Message

When it comes to communicating your leadership story, the most important concept is framing. This combines your message with your audience. The latter is discussed further in the next step. Framing allows you to provide context—to illustrate ideas and concepts in a particular way that gives them greater relevance, helps others to draw conclusions, and establishes a common understanding. As with the example above, you are not encouraged to walk around the office telling people aspects of your story, such as your humility. You would need to frame that message differently so that others could reach that conclusion.

Toni was a new partner at her firm. She had been hired from outside the organization. Toni inherited a new team of professionals eager to get to know her and her style. In her first team meeting, she took the time to discuss her professional background. Not only did she highlight where she worked, but she also highlighted what she had learned about leading people. And not all of her background was filled with successes. She admitted to the group that she had learned through some mistakes along the way. She talked about what was important to her as a leader—what her expectations were for herself and for her team. She shared some of her personal interests and also took time to answer questions. She let the team know that she would be scheduling individual meetings with each of them in the coming weeks to learn more about them.

In the book *Own the Room: Discover Your Signature Voice to Master Your Leadership Presence,* Amy Su and Muriel Wilkins discuss multiple ways of framing that you can adapt to fit your leadership story.[13] First, you can frame your story relative to where you fit with your company's bigger purpose and objectives. For example, you would establish a connection between where the team or organization is going and how you champion that. Second, you can frame your leadership story relative to a specific purpose or outcome. And third, you may want to illustrate your message through a story in order to bring it to life.

Your leadership story should be based on your experiences and beliefs. Your experiences and beliefs have to be front of mind for you. You should have data or examples that reinforce your leadership story or aspects of it.

Since you do not know and cannot plan for every situation that will lend itself to your telling your leadership story or elements of it, it is important for you to be prepared with the key messages you want to reinforce. Think about the following reflective questions.

REFLECTIVE QUESTIONS TO THINK ABOUT KNOWING YOUR MESSAGE

1. What, in your mind, are the most important aspects of your leadership story?
2. How would you best summarize who you are as a leader?
3. What are the inspirational aspects of your leadership story? What are the aspirational aspects?
4. What aspects of your leadership story would you like to further refine?
5. How can you build habits and routines around thinking about your leadership story and key messages?

Remember that stories help us to interpret the past in order to shape the future. For part of your message, you will want to clearly differentiate who you are as a leader from who you want to be. It is a subtle difference but an important one. This shifts you from a static mind-set to more of a learning and growth mind-set, and it adds a level of humility by assuming that you still have something to learn as a leader.

The anchor for telling your story lies in how well *you* understand, believe in, and connect to your own story. Additionally, you need your story to be relevant. We talk in the next part about knowing your audience, but it is important to point out here that there is a direct relationship between knowing your message, knowing your audience, and knowing the organizational context—or what the organization values. If your message is not aligned with either of these other two entities, your leadership story may be underappreciated or misinterpreted.

Bob's Struggle with Message

"Framing my message ... gosh, Tim. I am not sure I know the essence of my leadership message, let alone how to frame it for others," Bob said.

He was understandably frustrated. After all, he had been a project manager with a couple of direct reports. Right now, however, he is beginning to see that he has boxed himself in by being the lone ranger in companies that want to develop strategic leaders for initiatives that are bigger than an ordinary, short-term, let's-get-this-done-this-quarter kind of project.

"Tim, a couple of days ago you corrected me about elevator speeches—you told me that my leadership story is not some one-sentence elevator speech. OK, fill me in. Is it a paragraph, a page ... I just..."

"We are not talking words and punctuation here, Bob," I asserted. "We are talking about a grand vision. We are talking about an emotional jolt that makes people you lead say, 'Wow, I want to be part of that.' This is a flag, an anthem, and a battle plan all wrapped up in nontangible terms, not a bumper sticker or a project summary.

"Let me ask you a bold question," I continued. "Can you describe the grand idea you would like to implement and lead with a big, strategic team you choose and guide? What would it be like?"

"Well, I suppose I'd have to identify the type of people first," Bob began. "They don't all have to be in my profession, right? I can have a mixed, diverse group of people, not all with the same viewpoint?"

"Bob, this is a breakthrough. You've had something—something big—in mind for a while, haven't you? Now you have a reason to develop a leadership story. Or you might have an even longer résumé of employers from now until the next decade. Your choice, guy," I said smiling.

Quick Tips

To Know Your Message

1. Don't fabricate or misrepresent your leadership story.

2. Know the difference between who you are as a leader and who you want to be.

3. Rehearse your story and elements of it.

4. Read biographies and autobiographies of leaders. Note what made them great and how their story was told.

STEP 7

Know Your Audience

You are the first audience for your leadership story. Your job is to determine what is worth telling. Then, once you have filtered through and identified the most important aspects of your leadership story, the storytelling must become collaborative. It reinforces and bridges the relationship between you and your audience. And recall that your leadership story lives in the hearts and minds of others. Therefore, your audience plays an important role in your leadership story.

It is not simply about creating a bigger audience or one with more senior leaders. For example, if you are a first-time leader just starting out at a company, it may be unlikely that the president or CEO (or other senior leader) is in your immediate audience. So this chapter is less about increasing your audience and more about ensuring the significance of your message with existing audiences.

Stories need to be relevant to their audience. As your leadership story evolves, you need to be aware of how you fit with others and the organization. In other words, think about how your leadership story is aligned with and supports others. You need to identify who those in your audience are, what they want to know, why they should know it, and how and when to engage them. Keep in mind that the exchange should be two-way: as you give them information about your leadership story, seek to understand what is important to them at the same time.

Jessica met with her supervisor every other week. She used the same standard template for her updates that she used for her team. She listed the projects, their status, any accomplishments, and any barriers. Jessica was reporting on what she was comfortable with, what she would want to have known, and what she thought her supervisor wanted to know. He always nodded and made some notes, but he also routinely asked Jessica questions about the details of the financial statements. Sometimes Jessica was prepared and sometimes she was not. It gave her supervisor the impression that Jessica either wasn't informed or didn't care about the details, specifically the financial details that the supervisor cared very much about.

At her annual performance review, Jessica was surprised to be told that her inattention to these details was a negative. She had worked at the company for years, and this was the first time she had received this feedback. The expectations of the company and, more important, her supervisor had shifted. Once she realized that this was critical information for her supervisor and that she wasn't meeting expectations, Jessica revised her meetings to begin with a financial review and was prepared to answer any questions.

She also tried to incorporate this new revision into her regular team meetings. After the third meeting with her new financial review agenda item, she could sense that the group was shutting down. Outside of the meeting, Jessica asked one of her direct reports why the team was disengaged during the meetings. He said some of the team felt as if they were being beaten up in front of their peers. Furthermore, many of the details did not pertain to everyone in the room, so they were having a hard time following the conversation.

Although Jessica had been a leader at the company for over three years, she had an "aha" moment that brought her a new understanding. Up until that time, she had been providing the information that she thought was important. Her lesson in all of this was that leadership was not about her. She realized that the information her boss wanted was very different from what her peers needed. And both were contributing to her leadership story. For her boss, the story was about the extent to which Jessica understood the business and tracked the details. For her team, the story being written was that Jessica cared less about their accomplishments than she did about bottom-line details.

Identifying your audience is not the difficult part. The challenge, rather, is to determine what they already believe about your leadership story, their expectations, what they perceive as important, and how that aligns with your views. People in your audience will be looking to either hold up your leadership story against their expectations or validate their existing perceptions about your leadership story. In other words, they will look to make sense of what they know or perceive about you. Your job is to determine what is important to them. It is also helpful to know the organization's values and where you fit within the organization.

REFLECTIVE QUESTIONS TO THINK ABOUT KNOWING YOUR AUDIENCES

1. Who are your key audiences that you interact with most frequently?
2. Who are your most important audiences?
3. Which audiences' needs do you have the best understanding of? Which do you know least?

4.   What do people want to hear about your leadership story? What do they need to know? Why?

5.   What happens when your leadership story is not accurately represented to or by others?

When it comes to identifying your audiences, there are a few key groups that you should include: your direct reports, your supervisor, and your peers. Each of these groups has a different need around understanding your leadership story.

It is important that you identify the needs of each audience, and I would suggest that you leave little to chance when it comes to how others perceive your story. Interpretation can be the enemy of authorship. While some general needs are typically associated with each group, your challenge is to further identify your audiences and determine the specific needs within them.

To effectively communicate your leadership story to your audience, you need to show empathy and establish relevance. You need to be able to put yourself in their shoes. The best way to show empathy and know what is relevant for different audiences is to ask them. What is on their mind? What concerns do they have? What inspires and motivates them? Understanding this will allow you to frame your leadership story accordingly. Remember, this component of your leadership story is not about you; it is about them.

Although each audience is important in its own right, you should think about the frequency of your interaction with a particular audience and the importance of the message relative to that audience. Your message may be important, and there is more room for course correction in your story for those with whom you frequently interact. On the other hand, if you interact infrequently with an audience and the message to them is particularly important, you must be prepared and get the message of your leadership story right.

For your direct reports, you need to state your intentions as a leader. Refer back to "Step 1: Define Your Plot" for this. They should know what leadership means to you, what you value, and your expectations. They need to have a clear sense of where you are taking the team and how you intend to get there. They need to be motivated and inspired. And they need to be provided with feedback, be rewarded and recognized, and know how you will support their development.

Your supervisor needs to know how you will support her to accomplish her goals and the broader organizational goals. Refer back to "Step 4: Develop Your Theme" for this. In simple terms, she will want to know how you will get results. She will be keen on your capability to get the job done; how you handle organizational issues, challenges, and opportunities; whether you have executive presence; how you communicate with her and other leaders; and a variety of other possibilities. Your job is to determine what your supervisor wants and how you can best support her, even if you do not agree with her on everything. There is a concept called *managing up* that refers to how well you work with your supervisor and keep him or her informed.

Your peers will want to know how well you collaborate with and support them in achieving mutually dependent goals. Refer back to "Step 2: Identify and Build Strong Relationships with Your Key Characters" and "Step 3: Prepare for Conflict" for this. You will likely need to work differently with protagonists than you do with antagonists.

Keep in mind that there are other characters in your story who are neither protagonists nor antagonists. The point is that you have many audiences to consider, with differing needs and expectations of your leadership. You may very likely have to adapt over time and perhaps even modify your leadership in a variety of situations. This takes self-awareness in who you are as a leader.

In addition to knowing who your audiences are and what they care about, *how* you communicate with your various audiences is important. Technology has become a popular and sometimes useful means for communication. When it comes to your leadership story, communicating via technology, while fast and efficient, is one-dimensional. It tends to be literal and subject to the interpretation of the recipient. So when communicating aspects of your leadership story, is technology a friend or a foe? That is for you to decide. One suggestion to consider is that you should never communicate anything via technology that could elicit an emotional response.

Bob's Audience

"Tim, all along I thought audience meant the people I lead on something," Bob said.

"It does mean that," I asserted.

"OK, but during this session, you talked about different audiences, including the CEO. I am not leading upper management!" he claimed.

"Yes, you are—*if you are a successful leader,*" I said emphatically, playing with him a tad.

He had the eyes of a deer in the headlights. "So I have to know what a CEO wants in my leadership ability, and that might be different from what peers and direct reports need to know?"

"Precisely. In the last session, I asked if you have ever had a grand design you wanted to pull off. Most leaders have had a grand design. That's what leaders do. Now, whom do you think those leaders had to convince about those big, strategic initiatives? It wasn't just peers or potential team members. Those leaders spent days, weeks, pulling together proposals and cost analyses and PowerPoints, and then corralled the CEO and executive staff. Sure, the big guys could have said no, but they were risk takers too. And they sensed something. Their intuition about the leader kicked in. Bob, they, too, wanted to be led by leaders whose leadership story had cred and who had a history of pulling off big stuff. Get it now? Haven't you made proposals to the brass before?"

"Sure, I have. Sometimes they say yes, and sometimes they say no."

"No kidding? They sometimes say no? Bob, thanks for telling me that!" I said as we both laughed.

What Bob was getting is simple: Practice being a leader to all your audiences, and the yes rate might climb. Steeply.

Quick Tips

To Know Your Audience

1. Test the waters with select individuals by telling them aspects of your leadership story. Gauge their reaction to what you said and how you said it by asking for feedback. Afterward, don't necessarily change your message, but consider reframing it for that audience.

2. Find specific examples and stories of what constitutes successful leadership at your company.

3. Understand and/or define the vision of your company or team, and know how your personal mission supports the greater vision.

STEP 8

Maximize Moments of Truth

Life—and your leadership story—is made up of a series of moments. When there is something to be gained or lost, I call these *moments of truth*. Moments of truth are distinct opportunities to share or reinforce your leadership story. It is these events that make your leadership story memorable. To make your leadership story stick, your goal is for these events to be as positive and true to your leadership story as possible.

Let's say you are watching a basketball game. If you are asked to recall that game immediately afterward, you will probably remember a good number of details. Even so, you are not likely to remember every pass, shot, or dribble, even though they might have been important in the moment. As time goes by, you are likely to remember even fewer details. That's just how memory works.

On the other hand, in that same basketball game, you are likely to remember something amazing that happened—perhaps it was a slam dunk or shot at the end to win the game, or perhaps it was a missed shot. You are more likely to remember something out of the ordinary. Think of a moment of truth as a great awakening, a revelation that changes a significant part of your view of life. In short, a moment of truth is never momentary. It lasts. Long.

Relating this to your life and career, you might encounter only a few difference-making moments—or moments of truth—and they need to be maximized. How are you prepared for those moments? Are you sure that you will identify them as moments of truth, or will they just be momentary? Some may well be negative truths. And in the event that they don't go your way, how are you prepared to handle those moments? Do you learn from them so that you are better prepared for the next one?

Kevin is not one to talk about his accomplishments. He thinks that would sound as if he were bragging. So instead, he maintains a low profile and keeps the accomplishments of his team and his personal accomplishments to himself. When asked by his boss about updates, he shares some substantial accomplishments but does so in a rather bland way—as just part of a one-page bulleted weekly summary.

He has noticed that another team, led by Kristine, has been getting lots of kudos and recognition from leaders across the organization. Kevin wonders what the big deal is. Several months go by with a few more accolades for Kristine's team, and then the organization announces that Kristine and three members of her team are getting promoted for all the hard work they have done and their contributions to the business.

Timing is critical when it comes to building and communicating your leadership story. Good fortune favors the prepared. You have an opportunity—I would say an obligation—to be prepared and to be proactive in making the most of your moments of truth. Think about the following reflective questions to prepare for your moments of truth.

REFLECTIVE QUESTIONS TO HELP MAXIMIZE MOMENTS OF TRUTH

1. What are some specific opportunities for you to share your leadership story or aspects of it?
2. What do you see as your moments of truth?
3. How can you best be prepared for unanticipated opportunities to share your leadership story or aspects of it?
4. What are some additional opportunities for contact with key audiences?
5. How do you utilize moments of truth as a tool to learn and teach others?

Moments of truth can be planned or unanticipated, and they can be formal (e.g., meetings) or informal (e.g., chance encounters and casual conversations). Planned moments of truth can include events such as starting a new job, joining a new team or organization, one-on-one meetings, or presentations. The operative word here is planned. You see them coming, and you need to plan for them.

And even with these planned moments of truth, telling your leadership story can take on a number of variations, from subtle to direct. For example, if you are starting a new team or project, you have an opportunity to tell your leadership story. It may be to your advantage to be clear about your intentions and expectations as a leader.

Unplanned moments of truth can take on a number of forms. For example, you may have a chance encounter with a supervisor or colleague, or meet someone new at a professional conference. Not everything should be completely scripted by you.

Whether they are planned or unanticipated, being prepared for your moments of truth requires strong self-awareness and preparation. Those moments are an opportunity to reinforce and build upon your leadership story. They are an opportunity to clarify, inspire, and enlist other protagonists.

You are not necessarily looking for volume when it comes to these moments. In fact, you should be cautious about overcommunicating your leadership story or trying too hard. That may look like telling everybody everything all the time. Think quality of encounter over quantity.

You and your leadership story may be judged by your actions during these moments of truth as much as by your inaction. Are you cool and prepared? Or are you flustered? Do you speak up and offer insights, or do you sit back? What is important is to completely understand your message—your beliefs as a leader, as well as your capabilities and limitations. You need to anticipate the unanticipated.

But how do you do that? You need to constantly work on scenarios—those possibilities—in your mind. Go over them just as you would rehearse for an important presentation.

It is equally important to look at the dark side of this equation. Missed opportunities and lack of preparation for the unanticipated can set your leadership story back.

Ashley was a new leader I worked with. She very much wanted to impress her colleagues, her supervisor, and a key set of customers. She was always quick to volunteer to lead projects as a way to show her initiative and capabilities. She always said, "I got it," only to regularly fall short of expectations with missed timelines and projects that did not represent needs or expectations. While she believed she was being a great leader and showing great initiative, her narrative was being written and reinforced with every passing "I got it." Ashley had blown several moments of truth. Any single miss would not have reinforced this story, but over a relatively short amount of time, she became known across all of her key stakeholder groups as someone who did not get it.

The message for you? Set realistic expectations about who you are and your capabilities as a leader. You should underpromise and overdeliver. You can get in your own way and even derail your leadership story. Or, with preparation for and maximizing of moments of truth, you can be your own best champion.

Bob's Moments of Truth

Bob has had several moments of truth so far. He is picking up the cues for his leadership story, step by step.

"I am curious about something related to when you got this latest job," I began. "Did anyone on the interview team ask you something like "Bob, what's the biggest initiative you led?" or "Bob, what was the longest timeline you had for a project?"

"Yeah. I did get asked both of those questions, now that you mention it, Tim."

"You have just arrived at another moment of truth, Bob. They are expecting bigger things, and you can't wait any longer to write, direct, and act out your leadership story," I said firmly.

Quick Tips

To Recognize and Maximize Your Moments of Truth

1. Write out your headline prior to participating in key events (meetings, presentations, etc.).

2. Create your own moments of truth by getting actively involved in projects. Volunteer when you know you can exceed expectations that add value to the business or solve a challenging or complex problem. (Note: do not overcommit or overpromise.)

3. Have a prepared set of observations about ways you can improve the business. (Note: this is not about tracking a list of complaints, but about having genuine and realistic ideas for where you [and/or others] could improve the business.) Look for the right time and audience to share those ideas.

STEP 9

Actions Speak Louder Than Words

The language you use is a window into you, and so are your actions. You certainly need to be cognizant of what you and others say about your leadership story, but your actions are another very important way you express your leadership story.

As a leader, you are onstage virtually at all times. Your actions must align with your story. Your leadership story will be defined by your actions because others will be looking to validate their perceptions about leadership with your story. So, what you say, what you do, and your leadership presence are not three separate notions. Together, they make up your leadership story.

When your words and actions do not match, your credibility will suffer. The lack of credibility or consistency will then become part of your story.

Credibility refers to the alignment between what you say and what you do. Do you do what you say, and do people believe what you say?

A more important aspect of your leadership story is authenticity. *Authenticity* refers to the extent to which your beliefs are aligned with your words and your actions. It is a deeper connection and gets at the core of who you are as a leader. To increase authenticity, you again need to have a strong self-awareness of what you believe and value as a leader. "Step 1: Define Your Plot" provides the foundation for an authentic leadership story.

REFLECTIVE QUESTIONS TO THINK ABOUT THE ROLE OF ACTIONS AND OTHER NONVERBAL COMMUNICATION

1.   To what extent can people read your emotions?

2. What does your image—your style, attire, office space, etc.—say about you as a leader?

3. How does your attitude impact others around you?

4. How would you describe your executive presence? How would others describe it?

5. How might you boost your image?

When you want to focus on telling your leadership story, you need to be aware of the actions you take, as well as your nonverbal communication and presence. It all ties together. These aspects of your leadership story contribute to your confidence, image, credibility, and trustworthiness. For example, you cannot say that you have an open-door policy and then not be available. Or, you cannot say that you value collaboration and then not seek input from others. You cannot say that you value building strong relationships and then sit in your office all day.

I know a leader, Hannah, who was just beginning her role as a leader. Hannah would often say that she was a good leader. My response to her was, "Don't say you are a good leader. Go be a good leader." If great leadership requires you to inspire and motivate others, you need to actively engage others. Relationships, again, are key. Think about how you are physically present, visible, and available to your team. Think about whether you seek them out or they have to seek you out. Again, if there are particular aspects of leadership that are important to you—if you believe that they are essential for great leadership and a core part of your leadership story—you need to take actions that are consistent with those beliefs. For example, if being accessible is important to you, do you seek others out proactively or wait for them to come to you? Your actions speak volumes about how you value accessibility.

You need to be true to yourself. It may require operating outside of your comfort zone. Minimally, it will require a strong sense of self-awareness. You may think you are a good or great leader. If your actions do not support that, others are unlikely to perceive you that way, no matter how loudly and how often you proclaim it. As in the examples above, if you believe in building strong, collaborative relationships, you must take appropriate action. Walk around and get to know your team members.

Your leadership story will also exist in the hearts and minds of others relative to your leadership presence. Leadership presence is a choice. And since others are making judgments about you, you need to consider how you dress, how you keep your workspace, your body language, your expressions, your mood, your tone, and how you carry yourself. Do you appear as if you care or not? How does your style fit with the organization? You need to look around and make a determination.

Josh led a team of seven people, ranging from brand-new employees fresh out of school to seasoned veterans. No one questioned Josh's intelligence. And Josh capitalized on that with a saying, "It's what's in your head that matters, above all else."

That showed in other areas of Josh's life at work. His workspace was messy and appeared disorganized, although he claimed that he knew where everything was. While most leaders in the company wore pressed shirts and a sport coat, Josh frequently wore an untucked golf shirt. Many people laughed it off. Some of the more junior employees even emulated Josh's attire. They said, "Hey, it works for Josh."

Then two of Josh's peers were given additional leadership responsibilities—one was a straight promotion, and the other was a highly desirable project that Josh was as qualified to handle, if not more so. The project was going to have high visibility for the company, for the person leading it, and for the team working on it.

Josh went to his boss and asked why he had not gotten the opportunity, and his boss explained that while technical knowledge was a key consideration, it was not the only one. Given the project's visibility, it was equally important that the person leading this project reflect the company well through his or her professional demeanor.

Bob Balances Words with Action

"I don't get it, Tim. What Josh wore is unimportant. Hey, we've gone from casual Fridays to casual weeks in the last 10 years. And lots of creative people are quite disorganized. You know, it's the left-side, right-side brain stuff. Some people are logical, and others are intuitive and sometimes erratic," Bob said with some frustration.

"OK, Bob, let's put this in perspective. People make judgments, often subliminally or without thinking of fairness," I told him. "Put yourself in the big guy's chair. You're the big boss, and you have a choice for that big strategic initiative. If all things are equal, which person do you choose to lead it? The person with Post-it notes stuck all over the cubicle, with piles of papers on the floor, who often shows up looking like he slept in his clothes? Or the person who is not like that—keep in mind, all other things are equal—someone who doesn't trigger snickers. If you're the boss, you might have to spend time overcoming all kinds of objections, such as 'You sure you want that person running this thing?' All things equal, you go with the easy sell, Bob."

"But let's get back to me," he said. "I'm not any of those things."

"Maybe so, but actions speak louder than words. Given what you've told me, you apparently aren't very engaging with even your peer group, with whom you could interact, share, and solve common problems, encouraging and supporting each other. That lone ranger thing defines your leadership—or lack thereof," I told him with some hesitation.

Quick Tips

To Make Your Actions and Other Nonverbal Communication Speak Louder Than Words

1. Always look one level or more up in the organization to see how leaders dress, carry themselves, and keep their workspace. Model that and set the example.

2. Make a list of where you and others would rate you highly with regard to executive presence and where you need to improve. How do others view your presence? Write a specific plan for how you will improve your executive presence and create greater alignment.

3. Walk around and interact with individuals on your team regularly. Be sure to go to them and get to know them on a personal level, and see that they have the resources and support to get their job done.

4. If your actions and words ever do not align, recognize it and recalibrate your story or actions accordingly.

STEP 10

Enlist Others to Tell Your Leadership Story

Most leaders I work with are uncomfortable telling their leadership story. They feel it is too much like self-promotion. Whether you fall into this category or not, this step is for you because I have found those instincts to be mostly on point. You have to be careful about what you say about yourself versus what others say about you.

Because you have a vested interest in yourself, your leadership story is best handled through the words of others. If you sing your own praises, people may be skeptical or even resistant. They may look for ways to discount you or even contradict you. This chapter focuses on whom to enlist to tell aspects of your leadership story, how to enlist them, and why.

Pete was an extremely hard worker. He led a team of 14 professionals, and work required him to travel almost every month. Although it was logistically difficult to keep up with all the obligations of leading a team, it was a priority for Pete.

During one stretch, he was out of the office for nearly three weeks. One of the weeks involved a series of meetings that included Georgia, the company's senior vice president of marketing. In a casual conversation with Georgia, the topic came up that it was difficult for Pete to be away from his family and the team for any time, but this three-week run was particularly hard on him. Pete didn't complain about the travel; he simply stated that it was a long run.

The following week, while Pete was still traveling, Georgia was back in the office and at a meeting with the leaders of each of the departments. The subject of workplace flexibility came up, and a senior leader from another department said, "Have you noticed how much Pete has been out of the office? It seems like he is never here." Georgia replied,

"Now wait a minute. Pete is out of the office on work travel. He is working hard and committed to this company." Had Georgia not been in that meeting and spoken in Pete's defense, the story that may have been written was that Pete was out of the office, taking advantage of workplace flexibility. Instead, the story that was reinforced was that Pete was dedicated to the company and willing to make a sacrifice for it.

Recruiting Credibility Substitutes

Anyone you enlist to tell your leadership story acts as a credibility substitute. In his 1998 *Harvard Business Review* article "The Necessary Art of Persuasion," Jay Conger highlights the importance of credibility substitutes. He notes that credibility grows out of expertise and relationships, and credibility substitutes are trusted experts whose credibility becomes a substitute for your own.[14]

This reinforces the idea that whom you know—or rather who knows your leadership story—can be as important as what you know. When it comes to your leadership story, you can enlist credibility substitutes by taking initiative and volunteering to get involved with projects that you can do well, establishing strong relationships and showcasing your capabilities. But this takes time. I am reminded of the saying that it takes 100 acts to build trust and only one to tear it down. That holds true for credibility as well.

REFLECTIVE QUESTIONS TO THINK ABOUT BEFORE ENLISTING OTHERS TO TELL YOUR LEADERSHIP STORY

1. What is your comfort level in talking about your leadership story?
2. Who else might you enlist in telling your leadership story? Who are your credibility substitutes? Why?

3. What would you want others to say about your leadership story when you're not around?
4. How can you plant seeds with others for your true leadership story to grow?
5. How can you ensure that people within your team and organization know who you are and your capabilities as a leader?

Credibility substitutes are powerful because they have less of a vested interest or potential for bias, and they can vouch for you. Even with credibility substitutes, it matters who the sub is. If a senior-level leader who is respected across the organization tells your leadership story, it will benefit more than if an antagonist is telling it. It is best to have multiple, credible individuals supporting your leadership story. You have to let people get to know you, and you need to build relationships beyond the superficial for that to happen. The truth of the matter is, you have to make an effort.

A word of caution here: watch your motives for getting to know people and having them get to know you. If your motives are strictly for self-promotion, it rarely will work to your advantage. People see through that stuff. And it does not have to be all about how each other's weekend was. Your credibility substitutes will come from people who trust that you are going to help them, the organization, the department, and the team to look good. The truth is, people make judgments all the time. Some are conscious and some may be subconscious. But they are asking these basic questions: Can you be trusted with bigger responsibility? To get the job done? To reflect well on the organization?

There can be several sources of credibility substitutes when it comes to telling your leadership story. For starters, you need protagonists to tell your story. The protagonists you identified in "Step 2: Identify and Build Strong Relationships with Your Key Characters" provide a great start. These are people you identified who believe in you. They want to see you succeed.

Antagonists can play an important role as well. But you must reestablish your relationship with them and ensure that they accurately know key points of your leadership story. Since you have identified some initial potential antagonists, your job is to establish a more constructive relationship with them. You will best accomplish this through identifying common ground, establishing allegiances, and perhaps seeking first to understand their point of view while clarifying yours. You may not convert each antagonist to a protagonist, but the stronger the relationships you build, the better off you (and your leadership story) will be.

The role that others play in your story can best be illustrated with a story from outside of the business environment. A good friend of mine and a former colleague, Mary, told me this story, and it is a perfectly appropriate example of enlisting others to tell your story. She was part of a group of friends who periodically got together socially, usually involving food and lively conversation. There was a new person, Jackie, who had just become friends with others in the group. Mary had not yet had the chance to meet Jackie, but Jackie had been to several social events with some of the other friends. After one social event that Mary could not attend, a couple of friends told Mary that she just had to meet Jackie. Among other things, they said, Jackie made the best deviled eggs. A short time went by, and after another social event that Mary was unable to attend, she heard from several other friends, who said, among other things, that Jackie made the best deviled eggs. She asked whether they had all tried them firsthand, and to her surprise, only half of the people had tried them. Jackie had become known for outstanding deviled eggs even if people had not experienced them personally. It had become part of her story. A little time went by, and Mary had the opportunity to try Jackie's deviled eggs. She thought they were good. However, her expectations had been set so high, she concluded that Jackie's eggs were not any better than other deviled eggs she had had.

Bob Ponders Whom to Enlist

"How am I going to recruit these cred subs, Tim?" Bob asked. "I am new to this company."

"You need to change your sense of isolation, for one thing, Bob," I replied. "You need to embrace a sense of collegiality with peers. Get to know them. Start a lunch group with them, or meet for breakfast on, say, the first Friday of every month. Make it regular so that it's on their calendars. *Be the leader of your peers, starting next week!* With direct reports, do a one-on-one every week. Also, just drop in to chat ... 'Hey, how's it going?' Show people you understand their concerns about stuff. Listen ... and that doesn't mean you always must agree. If you listen, they will listen and understand what is on your mind. You don't have any antagonists at this place—yet—so don't sow the seeds of antagonism," I told him. "Plant your leadership. Take the initiative."

"I hear you ... I hear you," Bob said. And this time I think he began to understand the career crossroads, the opportunity, he was facing.

Quick Tips

To Enlist Others to Tell Your Story

1. Spend time getting to know people throughout the organization. Learn about who they are and what they do.

2. Ask others to describe what you are like when you are at your best.

3. Identify at least three credibility substitutes for you.

CONCLUSION

Leadership is a gift—a gift that requires you to set a direction; motivate, inspire, and develop others; and deliver results that matter. It is also a journey. It is about your experiences and the influence you have on others. Leadership is certainly about the work that gets done, but it is much more about how the work gets done and the relationships along the way.

A great story can motivate and inspire others. It can impart a message. Think about how your leadership story imparts a message, inspires, or motivates. Remember, your leadership story lives in the hearts and minds of others, and you are constantly onstage as a leader. Sometimes you can rehearse or plan ahead. Other times, improvisation is needed. Those around you will have expectations, assumptions, interpretations, and perceptions that impact your story. For you to be at your best, others' perceptions of you must be aligned with your story.

Consider that your leadership story has all the elements of a good story: plot, characters, conflict, theme, and setting. These are each instruments by which you can understand where you are aligned and where there is work to do on your story. No matter where you are in your journey, there is something to be gained by using the story as a framework to consider your past, present, and future. Understanding your leadership story provides a solid foundation for who you are, what you believe in, and what you value as a leader. It is a reminder of the important characters in your story, how you handle conflict, and what it takes for you to be at your best.

It is imperative that you be aware of what you believe about yourself and what others perceive as a path toward authenticity. Establishing that awareness will allow you to have greater ownership and alignment of your story. You can now better mitigate inaccuracies in your story, such as being perceived as insecure, arrogant, or unreliable ... or being overlooked altogether. You should be on your way to having greater control of your leadership narrative, or point of view. And you need to continue to challenge your own assumptions about what leadership means to you and how you will act as a leader. You need to continue to monitor your leadership story.

Understanding and taking authorship of your leadership story is not an easy task. It may require you sometimes to confront personal and interpersonal issues. It may require you to make tough decisions. Avoidance and inaction may be the easier path, but certainly the less fulfilling one. Additionally, if you don't recognize and understand your leadership story, you cannot communicate it or modify it. On the other hand, to the extent that you understand your story, you become the primary author of it. You can adjust your story and use it to energize and possibly even transform others.

Reviewing, reflecting, and understanding your leadership story may be the easy part of the process, relatively speaking. Action may be the toughest part. And, more important, turning actions into habits will be difficult. Habits require self-awareness, practice, and feedback. Turning actions into good habits has the potential to be transformational. What are you prepared to do to produce your best leadership story? What is your commitment to your leadership story?

After completing the activities in this book and having others complete activities, how do you feel about your leadership story? How has your mind-set about your leadership story shifted? Do you believe in yourself as a leader? Do you need to create a new story or perhaps simply refine some of the elements of your current story? Maybe you need to change the way your leadership story is perceived by others or possibly how it is communicated to others. Any of these actions require self-awareness and insights about what you are doing well, what you could do even better, what you are known for, and how you are perceived.

The good news is that your leadership story is dynamic. You can modify it. You have the opportunity to write and rewrite your leadership story. In fact, that is the mark of good leaders: they are aware of their leadership story and can make modifications as needed.

In addition to knowing your message, when it comes to communicating your story, you should know who your audience is, what their perceptions are, and what they want to hear. You should be aware of anticipated moments of truth and prepared for the unanticipated ones. There is more good news. You are not alone when it comes to communicating your leadership story. While it may be daunting to think that your story lives in the hearts and minds of others, if the right people have accurate perceptions of it, their role as credibility substitutes, champions, and ambassadors of your story can be quite powerful.

I hope that after reading this book, you are closer to understanding your leadership story and how others perceive it. That is essential for being the primary author in the narrative you intend—aligning who you are, what you believe in, and what you aspire to be with others' understanding of those things. I hope that you are able to find inspiration from within and can express that energy, enthusiasm, and authenticity to others—to help others grow, develop, and reach their full potential, and to help the team and organization do the same. I hope that you are able to make your leadership story an epic.

Bob's Epilogue: Five Years Later

Bob and I kept in touch over the years. I noticed that he had been with that new company now for five years. That got me curious, so I contacted him to suggest a lunch.

My challenge when we had first started meeting really got him thinking. He became the manager over all the project groups—all of them! He initiated what he called a lot of cross-pollination, a term I'd never heard him use before. "I've been pleased with how that opened up discussion and teamwork," he announced. "People aren't afraid to come up with out-of-the-blue ideas, even if some can't fly."

Two years ago, he proposed a major initiative that management approved. He's been holding semiannual team-unity meetings at an off-site conference center far from the city. The goal is to allow ideas to flow within the group.

Bob has been experiencing something else that's new to him. Often the top C-level execs will drift down to his office at the end of the day, sit down, and ask his opinion about company direction and problems. Far-reaching questions, what-if questions, the kind that executives don't ask of ordinary managers.

But Bob is no longer ordinary. At the crossroads, he took the road he had not taken before, the uncharted road leading to leadership, and he's apparently found it as fun as, if not more fun than, his lone ranger days in the corner cubicle.

So Bob went from one story to another, from shell shock about how he was being perceived to out-of-the-box proposals that got the big nod. He's fully embraced leadership as his new profession. He's learned from others.

He found a way to make jobs and careers transformational for his people. People want to be in his lead ... and they aren't building tepees! HR told him the sick-day rate in his division is the lowest in the company. People seem more energized than those he knew at past companies. Executives seek his opinion. He's provided some great direction. Bob recognizes now that his personal mission is to create leaders of the future.

The real message about one's leadership story is this: Your story continues to be written and revised as long as you have leadership responsibilities. It requires care and feeding. You must think about whether you are the primary author or others are writing it. Bob has that clear now.

Full disclosure here: Bob is a composite of many of my clients. If you have seen yourself in his questions and concerns, you have taken an important step in writing, directing, and acting in all the parts of your leadership story.

Enjoy—and prosper!

RESOURCES

The resources are provided to give you quick access to the activities, reflective questions, and tips from throughout the book. Although all of the parts of the book are meant to go together into a single process to understand and communicate your story, you may want to spend more time and effort on a particular aspect. That is perfectly OK.

Going through these resources is not meant to be an easy, skim-the-surface exercise. As you go through the various resources, the intent is that you take a deep look within to better understand who you are as a leader and become the primary author of your leadership story. Some of the activities and questions may be difficult. They may make you uncomfortable. You might even be tempted to gloss over them. But remember that the effort you give to these resources will directly impact what you get out of them.

Activities to Do Yourself

UNDERSTANDING YOUR LEADERSHIP STORY

Plot
Define Leadership
What Do You Value?
Solid Ground
Get Excited
You're on a Mission

Characters
Keys to Unlocking Connections
Common Ground
Monitor the Emotional Bank Account
Build Mentor Circles
Thank You!

Conflict
The I's Have It
What's Happening?
Learn from the Past, Commit to the
 Future
What It Takes
The Heart of Innovation

Theme
Give Yourself a Grade
Greatest Hits (and Misses)
Keep a Diary
Moving On
The Mirror

Setting
Masterful 2x2
Detour!
New Construction
Gratitude
Be Self-a-Where and S.M.A.R.T.

Activities to Give to Others

UNDERSTANDING YOUR LEADERSHIP STORY

Plot
Define Leadership
What Do You Value?

Characters
Keys to Unlocking Connections
Monitor the Emotional Bank Account

Conflict
Learn from the Past, Commit to the
 Future
What It Takes

Theme
Give Yourself a Grade
The Mirror

Setting
New Construction
Be Self-a-Where and S.M.A.R.T.

Reflective Questions

UNDERSTANDING YOUR LEADERSHIP STORY

Plot

What has been most rewarding in your career? Why?

What is your quest or challenge as a leader? Where and how do you want to make a difference/have impact?

What is important to you as a leader? Why?

What inspires and energizes you as a leader?

What would you like to accomplish as a leader?

Characters

With whom are your key relationships at work? Who impacts your ability to do your best work, and how do you impact others' ability to do their best work?

How can you build more supporters and champions of your leadership story than detractors?

What role do you play in your leadership story? Others? (Hero, villain, etc.) Why?

Who are your trusted advisors?

How would others describe you as a leader? How well is your leadership story aligned with others' interpretation of your leadership story?

Conflict

What have been recurring causes of conflict for you as a leader (e.g., types of tasks, people, situations)?

What is your role in conflict?

How do you typically react to, respond to, or handle conflict? How resilient are you? What would others say about how you handle conflict?

What is your approach, outlet, or mechanism for processing conflict constructively?

How do you resolve conflict? What impact does this have on your relationships? Your ability to get the job done?

Theme

What are you known for as a leader (skills, behaviors, attitudes)?

What do you want to be known for?

What are your strengths and areas for development as a leader?

What traits, behaviors, and characteristics are you most proud of as a leader?

How do you continuously develop yourself as a leader and teach others?

Setting

How does your setting enable or constrain your best leadership capabilities?

What gets rewarded and punished in your organization?

How have your travels shaped your perspective as a leader? Where have you been that has influenced your thinking?

How can you make the most of your current setting?

Where have you had the greatest impact and experienced the greatest satisfaction as a leader? Why?

THE ART OF COMMUNICATING YOUR LEADERSHIP STORY

Know Your Message

What, in your mind, are the most important aspects of your leadership story?

How would you best summarize who you are as a leader?

What are the inspirational aspects of your leadership story? What are the aspirational aspects?

What aspects of your leadership story would you like to further refine?

How can you build habits and routines around thinking about your leadership story and key messages?

Know Your Audience

Who are your key audiences that you interact with most frequently?

Who are your most important audiences?

Which audiences' needs do you have the best understanding of? Which do you know least?

What do people want to hear about your leadership story? What do they need to know? Why?

What happens when your leadership story is not accurately represented to or by others?

Maximize Moments of Truth

What are some specific opportunities for you to share your leadership story or aspects of it?

What do you see as your moments of truth?

How can you best be prepared for unanticipated opportunities to share your leadership story or aspects of it?

What are some additional opportunities for contact with key audiences?

How do you utilize moments of truth as a tool to learn and teach others?

Make Your Actions Speak Louder Than Words

To what extent can people read your emotions?

What does your image—your style, attire, office space, etc.—say about you as a leader?

How does your attitude impact others around you?

How would you describe your executive presence? How would others describe it?

How might you boost your image?

Enlist Others to Tell Your Story

What is your comfort level in talking about your leadershipstory?

Who else might you enlist in telling your leadership story? Who are your credibility substitutes? Why?

What would you want others to say about your leadership story when you're not around?

How can you plant seeds with others for your true leadership story to grow?

How can you ensure that people within your team and organization know who you are and your capabilities as a leader?

Tips

UNDERSTANDING YOUR LEADERSHIP STORY

Plot

You must know what you believe in and where you want to go as a leader in order for others to be inspired to follow.

Identify what inspires and energizes you about your work.

Sharing your point of view with others will increase accountability.

Characters

You can learn a lot from both good and bad leaders. Ask yourself what you would do the same as or differently than leaders you know have done.

Proactively build positive relationships and express gratitude.

Identify and seek input and guidance from trusted mentors.

Conflict

Conflict is inevitable. Perhaps more than results, how you react or respond to conflict or adversity will define you as a leader.

Find a mechanism or process by which you can deal with conflict constructively.

Be proactive in responding to conflict. It may not come naturally or comfortably, but if you can handle conflict well, it will greatly help your leadership story and build positive relationships.

Theme

For quick feedback, give yourself and others a grade; ask others to do the same. It can help initiate candid conversations, reinforce expectations, and highlight perceptions.

Effective leadership requires you to let go of (or delegate) some technical skills and embrace your role as a leader.

Reconcile how you think you are doing as a leader with how others perceive you are doing.

Setting

Take ownership and responsibility for
what you can do to make your setting
optimal for you.

Know and articulate what about a
setting enables you to be at your best
and constrains you from the same.

Actively seek feedback from your team
members about what it takes for them
to be at their best, and have a specific
plan to help support them.

THE ART OF COMMUNICATING YOUR LEADERSHIP STORY

Know Your Message

Don't fabricate or misrepresent your
leadership story.

Know the difference between who you
are as a leader and who you want to
be.

Rehearse your story and elements of it.

Read biographies and autobiographies
of leaders. Note what made them great
and how their story was told.

Know Your Audience

Test the waters with select individuals by telling them aspects of your leadership story. Gauge their reaction to what you said and how you said it by asking for feedback. Afterward, don't necessarily change your message, but consider reframing it for that audience.

Find specific examples and stories of what constitutes successful leadership at your company.

Understand and/or define the vision of your company or team, and know how your personal mission supports the greater vision.

Maximize Moments of Truth

Write out your headline prior to participating in key events (meetings, presentations, etc.).

Create your own moments of truth by getting actively involved in projects. Volunteer when you know you can exceed expectations that add value to the business or solve a challenging or complex problem. (Note: do not overcommit or overpromise.)

Have a prepared set of observations about ways you can improve the business. (Note: this is not about tracking a list of complaints, but about having genuine and realistic ideas for where you [and/or others] could improve the business.) Look for the right time and audience to share those ideas.

Make Your Actions Speak Louder Than Words

Always look one level or more up in the organization to see how leaders dress, carry themselves, and keep their workspace. Model that and set the example.

Make a list of where you and others would rate you highly with regard to executive presence and where you need to improve. How do others view your presence? Write a specific plan for how you will improve your executive presence and create greater alignment.

Walk around and interact with individuals on your team regularly. Be sure to go to them and get to know them on a personal level, and see that they have the resources and support to get their job done.

If your actions and words ever do not align, recognize it and recalibrate your story or actions accordingly.

Enlist Others to Tell Your Story

Spend time getting to know people throughout the organization. Learn about who they are and what they do.

Ask others to describe what you are like when you are at your best.

Identify at least three credibility substitutes for you.

NOTES

[1]   Dianna Booher, *Creating Personal Presence: Look, Talk, Think, and Act Like a Leader* (San Francisco: Berrett-Koehler Publishers, 2011).

[2]   The   Arbinger   Institute, *Leadership and Self-Deception: Getting Out of the Box* (San Francisco: Berrett-Koehler Publishers, 2010).

[3]   Steve   Arneson,   *Bootstrap Leadership: 50 Ways to Break Out, Take Charge, and Move Up* (San Francisco: Berrett-Koehler Publishers, 2010).

[4]   Jim Loehr, *The Power of Story: Change Your Story, Change Your Destiny in Business and in Life* (New York: Free Press, 2008).

[5]   Daniel   Goleman,   *Emotional Intelligence: Why It Can Matter More Than IQ* (New York: Bantam Books, 2005).

[6]   J.W. "Bill" Marriott Jr. and Kathi Ann   Brown,   *Without Reservations: How a Family Root*

Beer Stand Grew into a Global Hotel Company (New York: Diversion Books/LCP, 2014).

[7] John Zenger and Joseph Folkman, *The Extraordinary Leader: Turning Good Managers into Great Leaders* (New York: McGraw-Hill, 2009).

[8] Alan Gregerman, *The Necessity of Strangers: The Intriguing Truth About Insight, Innovation, and Success* (San Francisco: Jossey-Bass, 2013).

[9] Stephen Covey, *The 7 Habits of Highly Effective People: Powerful Lessons in Personal Change* (New York: Free Press, 1990).

[10] Carrie Perles, "Conflict Management Training Activities," eHow (March 2014), http://www.ehow.com/list_6738552_conflictmanagement-training-activities.html.

[11] George Orwell, *1984* (New York: Signet Classics, 1969).

[12] Nelson Mandela, *Long Walk to Freedom: The Autobiography of Nelson Mandela* (Boston: Back Bay Books, 1995).

[13]   Amy Jen Su and Muriel Maignan Wilkins, *Own the Room: Discover Your Signature Voice to Master Your Leadership Presence* (Boston: Harvard Business Review Press, 2013).

[14]   Jay A. Conger, "The Necessary Art of Persuasion," *Harvard Business Review* (May 1998).

ACKNOWLEDGMENTS

There is no way I could have completed this book without a strong support network. That begins with my wife, Sara, and our children, Finley and Chase. You are simply amazing. Words cannot describe how much I appreciate your support, patience, love, and encouragement. You are what is important in life. I love you and know that I could not have done this without you.

I also want to thank my mom, who has an amazing gift of patience, unconditional love, and support. You have always been my greatest fan, and that means a lot. Thank you also to Eddie and Ellie Sharpe, who show great interest and enthusiasm in my pursuits. Thank you for freely sharing your wisdom.

Walter McFarland is a person I admire and respect. I am very fortunate to call you a friend and mentor. You always see potential before I see it myself. Thank you for showing me the way. Thank you for listening and asking questions. I am a better person for knowing you.

To Jay Conger, I owe a big thank-you. You have contributed to my book and helped shape my thinking far more than you will ever know. Thank you for all your support and encouragement.

I owe a big thank-you to the GW ELP community for giving me so many opportunities and providing a strong foundation of knowledge for me to build on.

I've had the good fortune of working for some great companies with great leaders, colleagues, and team members. There are too many people to name, and I fear I might miss someone. But know that if you have been a colleague, I have learned from you. I have to mention that the first person I worked with on a big leadership project was Lori Zukin. Lori, thank you for being a great collaborator and teammate. Your depth of knowledge and willingness to share that knowledge started me off on the right foot, and I have never forgotten that. I have tried to pay it forward wherever possible.

And to my great bosses, thank you for providing me with opportunities, giving me feedback, and trusting me with greater responsibilities. I appreciate your having my back, encouraging me to pursue my interests, and allowing me to learn and grow. You never know what you are capable of until you take that first step. Thank you for allowing me to take many steps.

Thank you, Steve Arneson, for your insights and advice. Your enthusiasm for leadership is inspiring. And your guidance is appreciated. You are a great role model. Although you have done a lot more for me than make an introduction, I need to specifically thank you for making the introduction to Neal Maillet at Berrett-Koehler.

Neal and the rest of the Berrett-Koehler team are phenomenal across the board. They have each played a role in making this a really fun process. Neal has provided great feedback and perspective; thank you, Jeevan Sivasubramaniam, for making it quite a seamless process, always taking great interest in my ideas, questions, and concerns; thank you, Dianne Platner and your team, for your creativity and support on the book design; thank you, Linda Jupiter and your team, for making this a beautiful, reader-friendly book, and especially Elissa Rabellino, for your brilliant copyediting and suggestions; and to my reviewers, Kerry Radcliffe, Jan Nickerson, and Leigh Wilkinson, feedback is a gift, so I thank you for taking the time to offer such great feedback. I hope you see the difference you made.

Roger Peterson. You are great to work with. You have got a great gift when it comes to writing, and I appreciate the time you took and insights you shared to help bring my book to life.

As I reflect on how fortunate I am to have such a great group of people in my life, somehow "Thank you" doesn't seem to fully capture the gratitude I have. But I'll say it anyway. Thank you all for believing in me, encouraging me, and teaching me.

ABOUT THE AUTHOR

Tim Tobin is a learning and leadership professional committed to providing opportunities that help people reach their greatest potential. In his 25 years of professional experience, he has been directly responsible for the development of thousands of people, from C-level to first-time leaders, across multiple industries.

He believes that development must begin with self-awareness. He believes that we learn best through practice, and development should be an ongoing endeavor—one that is pursued with purpose. Another key to the development process in Tim's view is the interplay between action and reflection. In our action-oriented society, too often, we do not leave time to reflect. Too often, leadership is an afterthought. Not enough time is dedicated to thinking about leadership. This book was written to help facilitate your thought process about who you are as a leader and who you want to be, and to provide guiding actions to help get you to where you want to be.

Tim is currently vice president, global learning and leadership development, at Marriott International, where he is responsible for learning and leadership development strategy, programs, and curriculum across the enterprise. He has designed and delivered numerous leadership programs for a global audience. Here, Tim learned about team leadership and the importance of setting a strong vision, understanding the personal interests and development needs of each individual, and not simply leading the way you would want to be led. While at Marriott, he won the 2014 Chief Learning Officer award for Global Learning, the 2013 Bersin & Associates award for Enabling High Impact Learning, the 2012 Chief Learning Officer award for Innovative

Learning, and the 2012 Bersin & Associates award for Leadership Development Strategy Excellence.

Prior to Marriott, Tim was director at Baker Tilly (formerly Beers + Cutler), where he designed and implemented their corporate university and leadership strategy and programs. He was also responsible for their broader talent management functions. In this role, Tim realized the importance of building strong, collaborative partnerships across the organization. He introduced the Apprenticeship Model of Learning, implemented the company's first Learning Management System, and built their leadership strategy and programs. The resulting programs received multiple awards, including the 2010 Bersin & Associates Learning Leader award for Learning and Talent Initiative Excellence, the 2009 Helios HR Apollo award for outstanding employee development programs, and the 2008 Bersin & Associates award for Operational Excellence. He was also recognized with the Learning Leader award for outstanding service in support of Beers + Cutler.

Before Baker Tilly, Tim worked for Booz Allen Hamilton. In his role there, Tim had a broader human capital focus. It was there that Tim developed an appreciation for taking a consultative approach to work and the importance of understanding the needs of the business. He managed and participated in project teams focused on a variety of management, leadership, training, and human resource initiatives primarily for government clients. He was also a key contributor for a Booz Allen Hamilton Partner Development Program. While at Booz Allen Hamilton, Tim won the 2005 Future Human Capital Leader award from *Human Capital* magazine.

Tim received an EdD in human resources development from George Washington University, an MA in organizational management from the University of Phoenix, and a BA in psychology from the University of Delaware. He has been an adjunct professor for over 15 years at Catholic University, Trinity University, and George Washington University, where he has taught graduate and undergraduate courses in learning, strategy, and human-capital topics. He is currently a member of the University of Maryland Smith School of Business Executive Programs Advisory Board.

Tim is often a speaker at regional, national, and international conferences, and he has published in diverse publications such as *Sales and Service Excellence Essentials,* the *International Journal of Strategic Business Alliances, ASTD—The Torch, SmartCEO* magazine, and *Social Psychology and Education.*

On a personal note, Tim is an eight-time marathon finisher, a three-time Ironman triathlon finisher, and a finisher of the Great Chesapeake Bay Swim. He is a Washington, DC native. He lives there now with his wife, Sara, and their son, Finley, and daughter, Chase. You can contact Tim at ttobin7@gmail.com and stay connected on Twitter at @tobinleadersh ip.

Berrett–Koehler
BK Publishers

Berrett-Koehler is an independent publisher dedicated to an ambitious mission: *Creating a World That Works for All.*

We believe that to truly create a better world, action is needed at all levels—individual, organizational, and societal. At the individual level, our publications help people align their lives with their values and with their aspirations for a better world. At the organizational level, our publications promote progressive leadership and management practices, socially responsible approaches to business, and humane and effective organizations. At the societal level, our publications advance social and economic justice, shared prosperity, sustainability, and new solutions to national and global issues.

A major theme of our publications is "Opening Up New Space." Berrett-Koehler titles challenge conventional thinking, introduce new ideas, and foster positive change. Their common quest is changing the underlying beliefs, mindsets, institutions, and structures that keep generating the same cycles of problems, no matter who our leaders are or what improvement programs we adopt.

We strive to practice what we preach—to operate our publishing company in line with the ideas in our books. At the core of our approach is stewardship, which we define as a deep sense of responsibility to administer the company for the benefit of all of our "stakeholder" groups: authors, customers, employees, investors, service providers, and the communities and environment around us.

We are grateful to the thousands of readers, authors, and other friends of the company who consider themselves to be part of the "BK Community." We hope that you, too, will join us in our mission.

A BK Business Book

This book is part of our BK Business series. BK Business titles pioneer new and progressive leadership and management practices in all types of public, private, and nonprofit organizations. They promote socially responsible approaches to business, innovative organizational change methods, and more humane and effective organizations.

Berrett–Koehler
BK Publishers

A community dedicated to creating
a world that works for all

Dear Reader,

Thank you for picking up this book and joining our worldwide community of Berrett-Koehler readers. We share ideas that bring positive change into people's lives, organizations, and society.

To welcome you, we'd like to offer you a free e-book. You can pick from among twelve of our bestselling books by entering the promotional code **BKP92E** here: http://www.bkconnection.com/welcome.

When you claim your free e-book, we'll also send you a copy of our e-newsletter, the *BK Communiqué.* Although you're free to unsubscribe, there are many benefits to sticking around. In every issue of our newsletter you'll find

- A free e-book
- Tips from famous authors
- Discounts on spotlight titles
- Hilarious insider publishing news

- A chance to win a prize for answering a riddle

Best of all, our readers tell us, "Your newsletter is the only one I actually read." So claim your gift today, and please stay in touch!

Sincerely,

Charlotte Ashlock
Steward of the BK Website

Questions? Comments? Contact me at bkcommunity@bkpub.com.

Certified

B

Corporation
bcorporation.net